LOT 1

A LEGAL DECRIPTION OF JUDICIAL CORRUPTION
IN COOK COUNTY, ILLINOIS
COOK COUNTY PARCEL NUMBERS ARE NOT LOT NUMBERS

(Exhibits and videos are on the website www.frankjbarrett.com)

LOT 1

A LEGAL DECRIPTION OF JUDICIAL CORRUPTION
IN COOK COUNTY, ILLINOIS
COOK COUNTY PARCEL NUMBERS ARE NOT LOT NUMBERS

(Exhibits and videos are on the website www.frankjbarrett.com)

Frank J. Barrett

Library of Congress Control Number: 2023913003

ISBN: 978-1-960093-43-1   (Paperback)
ISBN: 978-1-960093-44-8   (eBook)

Printed in the United States of America

LOT 1

A LEGAL DESCRIPTION OF THE JUDICIAL CORRUPTION IN COOK COUNTY
THIS IS INCREDIBLY SIMPLE FOR ANYONE TO UNDERSTAND
COOK COUNTY PARCEL NUMBERS ARE NOT LOT NUMBERS

AS EVIDENCED in the filed record of an already vitiated 18 CH 13221, on June 19, 2019, at a hearing demanded by a Byline Bank and its Attorney Scott Kenig for the fraudulent procurement of a Receivership, Byline, and Kenig simply had a then absolutely clueless Cook County Judge Edward Robles FIX the actual genuine material legal description of our actual Property; for Robles to criminally aid and abet Byline and Kenig in the criminal, fraudulent foreclosure of our actual Property as criminally caused by Byline and Kenig; for Byline to criminally seize our actual Property for vastly below its actual market value of $580,000.00; by that then absolutely clueless Robles criminally entering the fraudulently fabricated by Kenig physically impossible THE COURT FINDS of Kenig as prepared by Kenig BEFORE that June 19, 2019 hearing as demanded by Byline for the fraudulent procurement of that Receivership.

THAT IS EXACTLY HOW IT IS DONE IN CHANCERY COURT
IN COOK COUNTY, ILLINOIS

As stated, on June 19, 2019, Robles was absolutely clueless as to what and why Robles was criminally FIXING for Byline and Kenig.

All that absolutely clueless Robles had to do on that June 19, 2019, was to say what Robles was told to say before that June 19, 2019 hearing as demanded by Byline for the fraudulent procurement of that Receivership; and then criminally enter whatever THE COURT FINDS of Kenig put in front of then absolutely clueless Robles by Kenig as already prepared by Kenig BEFORE that June 19, 2019 hearing as demanded by Byline for the fraudulent procurement of that Receivership; and that then absolutely clueless Robles never had to worry about being caught for doing so: NEVER:

Because the State of Illinois Appellate Court would simply PERFECT THE FIX a different way to find that we would have lost anyway:

And then the State of Illinois Supreme Court would simply refuse to hear the FIX.

That is exactly how all FIXES in Cook County always stay FIXED: ALWAYS.

However, that then absolutely clueless Robles had a very serious problem on that June 19, 2019.

Not only is Kenig an unconscionable pathological liar. Kenig is also an extremely stupid unconscionable pathological liar.

AS EVIDENCED in the filed record of that 18 CH 13221, by January 12, 2019, long before that June 19, 2019 hearing as demanded by Byline for the fraudulent procurement of that Receivership, Kenig had already ordered the preparation of the exact evidence of ail of Kenig's fraudulently fabricated physically impossible frauds upon the court, which could never have physically existed, which had already vitiated the entire proceeding of that 18 CH 13221 before that June 19, 2019 hearing as demanded by Byline for the fraudulent procurement of that Receivership; and the FIX of Kenig's THE COURT FINDS as already prepared by Kenig before that June 19, 2019 hearing as demanded by Byline for the fraudulent procurement of that Receivership; and then criminally entered by then absolutely clueless Robles was physically impossible and could never have physically existed: NEVER.

The picture on the cover of this Book, which was also an Exhibit of our DEFENDANTS' RESPONSE TO PLAINTIFF'S MOTION FOR APPOINTMENT OF RECEIVERSHIP already in the filed record for that June 19, 2019 hearing, as demanded by Byline for the fraudulent procurement of that Receivership, is of our actual single-story custom built 1600-1606 Westchester Boulevard, Westchester, Illinois.

That actual genuine material picture of our actual single-story custom-built 1600-1606 alone exactly evidenced ALL of the already criminal conspiracies to defraud Byline and Kenig, which had caused the criminal, fraudulent foreclosure of our actual Property; alone exactly evidenced ALL of Kenig's fraudulently fabricated physically impossible frauds upon the court, which could never have physically existed; and also alone exactly evidenced ALL of Robles's fraudulently fabricated FIXES which also could never have physically existed: NEVER:

1600-1606 is ONE mixed-use building

SEE: 1600-1606 Westchester Boulevard

Exhibit 1, which was Exhibit 1 of our DEFENDANTS' RESPONSE TO PLAITIFF'S MOTION FOR APPOINTMENT OF A RECEIVERSHIP already in the filed record before that June 19, 2019 hearing as demanded by Byline for the fraudulent procurement of that Receivership, are the actual genuine material Plat of Survey and the actual genuine material Warranty Deed with the actual genuine material legal description of our actual Property:

Lot 1 in George F. Nixon & Company's Central Addition to Westchester, being a Subdivision of the North 12 acres of the West half of the Southwest quarter of Section 21, Township 39 North, Range 12 East of the Third Principal Meridian in Cook County, Illinois.

Our actual single-story custom built totally attached 1600-1606 Westchester Boulevard has always been entirely located on that 100-foot-wide Lot 1: ALWAYS.

Our actual detached 6-car residential Brick Garage has always been located on those parts of Lot 3 and Lot 5: ALWAYS.

SEE: 1600=1606 Westchester Boulevard

AS EVIDENCED by Kenig in the filed record before that June 19, 2019 hearing as demanded by Byline for the fraudulent procurement of that Receivership, our actual Property has always consisted solely of only that 100-foot-wide Lot 1 and those parts of Lot 3 and Lot 5: ALWAYS.

Kenig had already exactly evidenced all of Kenig's criminal absurd, fraudulently fabricated, physically impossible frauds upon the court, which could never have physically existed, before Kenig even committed Kenig's criminal absurd physically impossible frauds upon the court, which could never have physically existed: NEVER.

AS EVIDENCED in the filed record, first Byline, and Kenig and that then now collusive Robles have now criminally conspired for years to forever fraudulently deny that Lot 1 ever even existed; for Byline and Kenig to cause the criminal, fraudulent foreclosure of our actual Property; for Byline to criminally seize our actual Property for vastly below its actual market value of $580,000.00.

THAT IS THE FIX OF 18 CH 13221

Simply have that then absolutely clueless Robles on that June 19, 2019 FIX that exact "Lot 1 in George F. Nixon & Company's Central Addition to Westchester, being a Subdivision ..." out of existence; to criminally aid and abet Byline in the criminal, fraudulent foreclosure of our actual Property, as caused by Byline and Kenig; for Byline to criminally seize our actual Property for vastly below its actual market value of that $580,000.00.

COOK COUNTY PARCEL NUMBERS ARE NOT LOT NUMBERS

Exhibit 2, and in the filed record of that CH 13221, is the actual genuine material "as built" blueprint of our actual single-story custom-built totally attached 1600-1606 Westchester Boulevard as on file with the Westchester Fire Department:

Our actual single-story Westchester Medical Center, 1600, has always been totally physically attached and united by an interior masonry foundation wall; physically attached and connected by an interior common wall/ masonry fire barrier; and joined by a custom-built interior door to our actual personal residence, 1606, as an inseparable permanently bound and contained under one roof as:

"1600-1606 is ONE mixed-use building."

SEE: 1600=1606 Westchester Boulevard

AS EVIDENCED, first Byline and Kenig and then a now collusive Robles will forever fraudulently deny that:

1600-1606 is ONE mixed-use building."

But it was always:

TWO FRAUDULENTLY FABRICATED, PHYSICALLY IMPOSSIBLE SEPARATE BUILDINGS

SEE: 1600-1606 Westchester Boulevard

Exhibit 3 is the exact reason for the already criminal conspiracy to defraud Byline and Kenig to cause the fraudulent foreclosure of our actual Property; it is the exact reason for all of Kenig's fraudulently fabricated physically impossible frauds upon the court, which could never have physically existed; and is also the exact reason of then all of absolutely clueless Robles's fraudulently fabricated physically impossible FIXES, which also could never have physically existed: NEVER.

Exhibit 3, and in the filed record of that 18 CH 13221, is the actual genuine material 2017 Cook County Treasurer Second Installment Property Tax Bill for our actual Property Index Number 15-21-301-206-0000, which use for property taxation purposes, is our actual single-story attached Westchester Medical Center, as published and provided to Byline on July 3, 2019, by the Cook County Treasurer:

FACTS		**FIX**	
Cook County Assessor		Byline/ Kenig / Robles	
1600-1606 is ONE mixed-use building		TWO SEPARATE BUILDINGS	
2016 Total Tax: $18,380.95		2016 Total Tax: $18,380.95	
Classification 2-12		Classification 517	
TOTAL PAYMENT DUE		TOTAL PAYMENT DUE	
$0.00		$9,279.15	
2016 Assessed Value	$63,025	2016 Assessed value	$63,025
2107 Property Value	$290,190	2017 Property Value	$290,190
2107 Assessment Level	x 10%	2017 Assessment Level	x 25%
2017 Assessed Value	29,019	2017 Assessed Value	72,547
2017 Total Tax	$6,643.29	2017 Total Tax	$19,388.67

AS EVIDENCED in that filed record of that already vitiated 18 CH 13221, first Byline and Kenig and then now collusive Robles forever fraudulently denied that our actual single story 1600-1606 was ever "1600-1606 is ONE mixed-use building" but was always TWO FRAUDULENTLY FABRICATED PHYSICALLY IMPOSSIBLE TWO SEPARATE BUILDINGS; to precisely forever fraudulently deny that PARCEL 206 was ever reclassified by the Cook County Assessor as Classification 2-12 to be assessed at 10% of market value but was always Kenig's fraudulent misclassification of Classification 517 to be assessed at 25% of market value; to forever fraudulently deny that the TOTAL PAYMENT DUE was ever $0.00 but was always a fraudulently fabricated TOTAL PAYMENT DUE of $9,279.15; to forever fraudulently deny that the 2016 Assessed Value of that $63,025 was ever reduced to that 2017 Assessed Value of that $29,019 but had instead increased to that fraudulently fabricated 2017 Assessed Value of that $72,547; to forever fraudulently deny that the 2016 Total Tax of that $18,380.95 was ever reduced to that 2017 Total Tax of that $6,643.29 but had instead increased to that fraudulently fabricated 2017 Total Tax of that $19,388.67; to forever fraudulently deny that Byline and Kenig had caused the fraudulent foreclosure of our actual Property; because our actual single-story custom built totally attached 1600=1606 as always located on Lot 1 was always first Byline's and Kenig's and then Robles's:

TWO FRAUDULENTLY FABRICATED, PHYSICALLY IMPOSSIBLE SEPARATE BUILDINGS

SEE: FACTS/FIX

SEE: 1600-1606 Westchester Boulevard

SEE: Lot 1

PROPERTY INDEX NUMBER

Only the Cook County Assessor is authorized, pursuant to statute, to classify real property in Cook County for property tax purposes pursuant to the actual use of the property.

A PIN (Property Index Number) is a numerical code for the legal description of a piece of land as it has been defined for real estate taxation purposes. The formatted code points to a parcel's location on the Cook County property tax maps.

The eighth, ninth, and tenth digit of every PIN is always a PARCEL NUMBER: ALWAYS.

Cook County Clerk's Office

Parcel and lot are often used interchangeably, but there is a difference. Simply stated, a parcel is an identification for taxation purposes, whereas a lot is a legally recognizable subdivision of property with a legal description that specifies developmental permissions and restrictions.

COOK COUNTY PARCEL NUMBERS ARE NOT LOT NUMBERS

Pursuant to the Cook County Assessor Definition of Codes for Classification of Real Property:

Class 201: residential garage

Class 203: single-story residence, any age, 1,000 to 1,800 square feet

Class 2-12: mixed-use commercial/residential building with apartment and commercial buildings totaling less than six units or less with a square footage of less than 20,000 square feet

SEE: FACTS/FIX

Class 517: one-story commercial building

SEE: FACTS/FIX

Pursuant to Cook County Ordinance for Assessment Level:

Class 201 is assessed at 10% of the estimated market value.

Class 203 is assessed at 10% of the estimated market value.

Class 2-12 is assessed at 10% of the estimated market value.

SEE: FACTS/FIX

Class 517 is assessed at 25% of the estimated market value.

SEE: FACTS/FIX

Exhibit 4 and as evidenced in the record by Kenig before that June 19, 2019 hearing as demanded by Byline for the fraudulent procurement of that Receivership, is the actual genuine material Sidwell Cook County property tax map for our actual Property:

AS EVIDENCED by Kenig, our actual single-story Westchester Medical Center, 1600, is located on the North 66.77 feet of Lot 1 and on PARCEL 206 for property taxation purposes; our actual attached single-story personal residence, 1606, is located on the continuous South 34.23 feet of Lot 1 and on continuous Parcel 207 for property taxation purposes; and our actual detached six-car residential garage is located on those parts of Lot 3 and Lot 5 and on Parcel 209 for property taxation purposes:

COOK COUNTY PARCEL NUMBERS ARE NOT LOT NUMBERS

Then the forever fraud upon the court of Kenig, which will then become the forever FIX of Robles, is that Lot 1 never even existed.

Exhibit 5, and in the filed record, is the 2016 Cook County Treasurer Second Property Tax Bill for PARCEL 206, which use for property taxation purposes, is our actual single-story attached Westchester Medical Center, 1600.

The 2016 Classification of PARCEL 206 was 517 single-story commercial buildings to be assessed at 25% of market value; the 2016 Assessed Value of PARCEL 206 was $63,025; and the 2016 Total Tax of PARCEL 206 was $18,380.95.

On February 13, 2018, the Cook County Assessor will admit that: THE CLASS WAS INCORRECT BASED ON THE USE OF THE PROPERTY.

That "PROPERTY" is Lot 1.

Exhibit 6 and in the filed record is the 2016 Cook County Treasurer Property Tax Bill for our actual continuous Property Tax Index Number 15-21-301-207-0000 (PARCEL 207), which use for property taxation purposes, is our actual single-story personal residence, 1606.

The 2016 Classification of PARCEL 207 was Class 203, one story residence to be assessed at 10% of market value; the 2016 Assessed Value of PARCEL 207 was $150,200; and the 2016 Total Tax for PARCEL of 207 was $2,921.55.

On February 13, 2018, the Cook County Assessor will admit: THE CLASS WAS INCORRECT BASED ON THE USE OF THE PROPERTY.

That "PROPERTY' is Lot 1.

Over the years, we received letters from numerous tax attorney associations stating that income property should not be taxed at more than 20% of gross income.

For years we were being taxed at 35% to 38% of the gross rentals of our actual single-story attached Westchester Medical Center. We filed three Certificates of Error with the Cook County Assessor to have the real estate taxes for PARCEL 206 be adjusted to 20% of the gross rentals of our actual single-story Westchester Medical Center, 1600, all to no avail. Twice our Certificates of Error for such were lost, and the third was denied.

Classification 2-12

In the first week of August 2017, I called Raila & Associates, a professional real estate tax attorney association, and spoke with a Nancy Todd and explained such.

Ms. Todd told me that Raila could probably not have the property tax for PARCEL 206 reduced to 20% of the gross rentals of our Westchester Medical Center but could probably have the real estate tax for PARCEL 206 reduced to 22% of those gross rentals because of the horrendous vacancy rate of office space in Proviso Township and then Raila would file Certificates of Error for 2014, 2015 and 2016 for the same reason for property tax refunds from the Cook County Treasurer.

We agreed because 22% was a lot better than 35% to 38%.

I downloaded Raila's forms; submitted the actual Plat of Survey of our actual Property as the Site Locator Map; provided the rent roll for the four tenants; and 2014; 2015; and 2016 Schedule is for our single-story Westchester Medical Center, 1600, and submitted such to the intake department of Raila and such was accepted.

On that day in the first week of August 2017, the pictures of PARCEL 206 and continuous PARCEL 207 on the Cook County Assessor Website were identical:

Pursuant to those two identical pictures:

1600-1606 is an inseparable, permanently bound, and contained under one roof as:

"1600-1606 is ONE mixed-use building."

SEE: 1600-1606 Westchester Boulevard

Exactly because of those two identical pictures and the actual Plat of Survey for our actual Property, Ms. Todd called the next morning:

"Congratulations Mr. Barrett, your property is a classic RCL 2-12. We can save you at least $10,000.00 in real estate taxes for 2017, and when that is accepted, Raila can get you at least $30,000.00 in refunds for the years 2014, 2015, and 2016 from the Cook County Treasurer.

Ms. Todd explained to me that our Westchester Medical Center was not one mixed-use building and our personal residence was not one mixed-use building, but that our Westchester Medical Center with its four tenants totally attached to our personal residence is one mixed-use building to be assessed at 10% of market value.

Ms. Todd proposed that Raila file an RCL 2-12 to have PARCEL 206 be correctly reclassified from Class 517, a one-story commercial building being assessed at 25% of market value, to Class 2-12, a mixed-use commercial/residential building to be assessed at 10% of market value; and to have continuous PARCEL 207 also be correctly reclassified from Class 203, one story residence being assessed at 10% of market value to Class 2-12, mixed-use commercial/residential building to still be assessed at 10% of market value based upon the actual use of Lot 1.

We agreed.

Exhibit 7 and submitted as an Exhibit for us in the filed for that June 19, 2019 hearing, as demanded by Byline and Kenig for the fraudulent procurement of that Receivership, is the Cook County Assessor standard BUILDING RECORD RESIDENTIAL as dated September 5, 2017, for the internal inspection of 1606, our personal residence, with a diagram of our Westchester Medical Center, 1600, totally attached to our personal residence, 1606:

Per internal inspection, there is a door joining residential unit to com. unit.

PRO RATION BREAKDOWN
70% TO PAR 206
30% TO PAR 207
% TO PAR
Q-UP 2-12 4068

First, Byline and Kenig and then Robles will forever fraudulently deny that the Cook County Assessor ever determined for property taxation purposes:

Q-UP 2-12 4068 #

Six car garage is on Parcel – 009

DOC 113329

It is not uncommon in Cook County for a building to be on more than one continuous parcel for property taxation purposes—that standard Cook County Assessor form provided for such.

DOC 113329 was our 2017 Assessment Appeal Number for PARCEL 206 and continuous PARCEL 207.

By a May 8, 2018 letter, Kenig had already denied that our actual 2017 Assessment Appeal Number 0113329 for PARCEL 206 and continuous PARCEL 207 ever existed and denied that September 5, 2017, internal inspection of our actual single story 1600-1606 by the Cook County Assessor ever occurred.

By that same May 8, 2018 letter, Kenig had already denied that 1600 was ever attached to 1606.

Then Kenig's forever fraud upon the court is that 206 and 207 were never PARCEL NUMBERS but were always separate and distinct LOT NUMBERS to forever fraudulently deny that Lot 1 ever existed.

COOK COUNTY PARCEL NUMBERS ARE NOT LOT NUMBERS

At that June 19, 2019 hearing, when our Attorney argued that the property taxes for our actual Property had been reduced, Robles's answer was:

"So what."

Pursuant to that inspection of our actual Property by the Cook County Assessor, Exhibit 8 and in the filed record of that already vitiated 18 CH 13221 is the October 9, 2017 letter from the Cook County Assessor:

2017 Assessment Appeal

Township: PROVISO

Appeal Number: 0113329

Property Index Number (s):

15-21-301-206-0000

15-21-301-207-0000

By that May 8, 2018 letter, Kenig will forever fraudulently deny that our actual 2017 Assessment Appeal Number 0113329 for PARCEL 206 and continuous PARCEL 207 as filed with the Cook County Assessor ever even existed.

I am pleased to inform you that our appeal department has reviewed your appeal and determined that the assessed valuation of your property should be reduced. Your new assessed value is indicated below. This is a result of a change in classification.

This is a result of a change in classification.

By that same May 8, 2018 letter, Kenig will specifically forever fraudulently deny that there was ever any reduction in the assessed value of PARCEL 206 and forever fraudulently deny there was ever any change in the classification of PARCEL 206 and continuous PARCEL 207.

The reduction will be reflected on the second installment of your 2017 real estate tax bill, payable in 2018.

ORIGINAL CLASS	PROPERTY INDEX NUMBER	2016 PRIOR ASSESSED VALUE	PROPOSED 2017 ASSESSED VALUE	2017 CURRENT AV
517	15-21-301-206-0000	63,025	79,758	29,019
203	15-21-301-207-0000	15,020	18,051	12,048

By that same May 8, 2018 letter, Kenig will forever fraudulently deny that the 2017 CURRENT AV of PARCEL 206 was ever that $29,019:

SEE: FACTS/FIX

Ms. Todd called to explain that letter.

The decision of the Cook County Assessor on our 2017 Assessment Appeal Number 0113329 would not become Final until Proviso Township was Certified by the Cook County Assessor.

When that happened, then Raila would file six Certificates of Error for PARCEL 206 and continuous PARCEL 207 for the years 2014; 2015; and 2016 for refunds from the Cook County Treasurer,

The changes in classification to Class 2-12 for PARCEL 206 and continuous PARCEL 207 would be evidenced on the 2017 Cook County Treasurer First Installment Property Tax Bills due on March 1, 2018.

And the reductions in the Assessed Values of PARCEL 206 and continuous PARCEL 207 would be evidenced on the 2017 Cook County Treasurer Second Installment Property Tax Bills due then on September 1, 2018.

REQUIRED LOW-POINT BALANCE

PARCEL 207, which use for property taxation purposes is our actual single-story attached personal residence, 1606, was the collateral for Loan # 11147245, which would expire in September of 2018.

PARCEL 206, which use for property tax purposes, is our actual single-story attached Westchester Medical Center, 1600, and PARCEL 209, which use for property tax purposes, is our actual detached residential garage, were the collateral for Loan # 11147585, which was also to expire in September of 2018.

Exhibit 9 in the filed record is Byline's ANNUAL ESCROW DISCLOSURE STATEMENT for Loan #11147585 as dated October 31, 2017, with PARCEL 206 stilt incorrectly classified as Class 517 to still be incorrectly assessed at 25% of market value and a 2016 Assessed Value of $63,025:

YOUR NEW PAYMENT INFORMATION

PRINC & INT	$1,455.55
ESCROW PMT	1,671.45
DATE 1/16/18	$3,127.00

CURRENT TAX ESCROW PROJECTION
PROJECTED PAYMENTS FROM YOUR ESCROW THIS CYCLE

TAXES	COOK COUNTY	1st INST	10,669.13
TAXES	COOK COUNTY	2nd INST	8,981.32
			19,650.45

By that same May 8, 2018 letter, Kenig will fraudulently deny that the word PROJECTED ever appeared on that document prepared by Byline.

Pursuant to statute, we had to pay 55% of the then 2016 property taxes for PARCEL 206 and PARCEL 209 for the first installment due on March 1, 2018.

MONTH	PAYMENTS TO ESCROW	PAYMENTS FROM ESCROW DESCRIPTION	ESCROW BALANCE
8/18			12256.4
8/18			3275.08 RLP

(RLP) YOUR REQUIRED LOW-POINT BALANCES

ONLY AFTER Byline and Kenig had caused the criminal foreclosure of our actual Property did Kenig provide evidence in the filed record that we always maintained that REQUIRED LOW POINT BALANCE of that $3,275.08 during the pendency of Loan #11147585.

AS SUCH, under the actual provisions of Loan #11147585, after our February 16, 2018, payment of $ 3270.00 to Byline, Byline could never, and never did, demand any more monthly escrow payments and could never, and never did, declare any default in our property tax escrow account for Loan #11147585, as would be admitted by Byline on April 18, 2018.

NOVEMBER 18, 2017

Exhibit 10, and in the filed record, is the Cook County Assessor's Final decision on our actual 2017 Assessment Appeal Number 0113329 for PARCEL 206 on its Website as of November 18, 2018:

Status:
Status Date:
Prior Value   **63,025**
Current Value   **29,019**

As of that November 18, 2018, PARCEL 206 was correctly reclassified from Class 517, a one-story commercial building assessed at 25% of market value, to Class 2-12, a mixed-use commercial/residential building to be assessed at 10% of market value; and the 2016 Assessed Value of $63,025 was adjusted to a 2017 Current Assessed Value of $29,019 due to that change in classification.

SEE: FACTS/FIX

Exhibit 11, and in the filed record, is the Cook County Assessor Final decision on our actual 2017 Assessment Appeal Number 0113329 for our continuous PARCEL 207 on its Website as of November 18, 2017:

As of that November 18,2017 continuous PARCEL 207 was also correctly reclassified from Class 203, single story residence, also to Class 2-12, mixed use commercial/residential building to still be assessed at 10% of market value.

Upon the Cook County Assessor granting our 2017 Assessment Appeal Number 013329, Raila filed six Certificates of Error for PARCEL 206 and continuous PARCEL 207 for the years 2014, 2015, and 2016 for property tax refunds from the Cook County Treasurer.

Byline and Kenig never claimed that the Cook County Assessor had erred in correctly reclassifying PARCEL 206 and continuous PARCEL 207 as Class 2-12 to be assessed at 10% of market value and never claimed that Byline was ever harmed by the Cook County Assessor doing so.

INSTEAD, by that May 8, 2018 letter, Byline, and Kenig forever fraudulently denied that our actual 2017 Assessment Appeal Number 0113329 for PARCEL 206 and continuous PARCEL 207 ever even existed and was ever granted by the Cook County Assessor; to specifically forever fraudulently deny that PARCEL 206 was ever Class 2-12 to be assessed at 10% of market value but was always Kenig's fraudulently misclassified Class 517 to be assessed at 25% of market value; to forever fraudulently deny that the 2017 Current Assessed Value of PARCEL 206 was ever that $29 019; for Byline and Kenig to use Kenig's fraudulent misclassification of PARCEL 206 to cause the fraudulent foreclosure of our actual Property:

SEE: FACTS/FIX

Exhibit 12, and in the filed record, is my November 18, 2018, e-mail to Byline Loan Officer Rosemarie Viramontes:

HI ROSEMARIE:

ON THE COOK COUNTY ASSESSOR WEBSITE, APPEAL HISTORY CHECK/STATUS

15-21-301-206-000 FOR OUR OFFICE

2016	2017
FINAL	FINAL
63,025	29,019

15-21-301-207-000 FOR OUR HOME

2016	2017
FINAL	FINAL
15,020	12,848

By that May 8, 2018 letter, Kenig will admit that a Certificate of Error was filed for us with the Cook County Assessor, but never for PARCEL 206 and continuous PARCEL 207.

By that same May 8. 2018 letter, Kenig will forever fraudulently deny that I ever informed Byline of the Cook County Assessor Final November 18, 2017 decision on PARCEL 206 to forever fraudulently deny that the 2017 Assessed Value of PARCEL 206 was ever $29,019:

SEE: FACTS/FIX

BOTH OF MY REAL ESTATE TAX BILLS WILL GO DOWN SIGNIFICANTLY.

The actual market value of our actual Property would increase just as significantly.

That, of course, is the exact reason for 18 CH 13221.

On October 23, 2018 when Kenig filed Byline's fraudulent COMPLAINT FOR FORECLOSURE AND OTHER RELIEF for Loan #11147585, the actual outstanding balance of our two actual Loans with Byline was approximately $400,000.00.

On that same October 23, 2018 to be admitted by Kenig the actual market value of our Property was $580,000.00.

Why would Byline ever want to renew our two actual Loans for approximately $400,00.00 when Kenig could cause the criminal fraudulent of our actual Property for Byline to criminally seize our actual Property for vastly below that actual market value of that $580,000.00 and Kenig could receive Kenig's substantial legal fees for doing so?

Pursuant to the actual provisions of Loan #1117585, even though no monthly escrow payments could ever be **"required"** and never were **"required"** of us by Byline after our February 16, 2018 payment of $3.271.00 to Byline, we still proposed to pay Byline $500.00 per month in hopes of retaining that below-market 4% Loan for Loan #11147585.

We tried playing nice on that November 18, 2017.

On Monday, Viramontes called me to tell me that a Mark Hansen was now our new Loan Officer and that she was absolutely thrilled for us in acquiring that 2017 Assessed Value of $29,019 for PARCEL 206.

On that Monday, I forwarded that same November 18, 2017, e-mail to Hansen:

"Thank you, Mr. Barrett."

Hansen called twice that week to determine which PARCELS went with which Loans and Hansen was also absolutely thrilled for us receiving that 2017 Assessed Value of that $29,019 for PARCEL 206.

Hansen was a very courteous gentleman: WAS.

Exhibit 13 is Hansen's November 18, 2017, e-mail to myself:

Mr. Barrett, I have asked our escrow department to manually re-run the escrow analysis based on the information you provided. I will provide you with an update as soon as that is completed.

Thank you for your patience.

On October 31, 2017, with PARCEL 206 still being incorrectly classified as Class 517 to still be assessed at 25% of market value and the 2016 Assessed Value of PARCEL 206 still being $63.025, pursuant to the then existing 2016 Cook County Treasurer records the **"projected"** second installment tax bill for Loan #1147585 due then on September 1, 2018, was: $8,981.32.

As of November 18, 2017, with PARCEL being Class 2-12 and the 2017 Assessed Value being $29,019, pursuant to the then existing 2016 records of the Cook County Treasurer, the **"projected"** second installment property tax bill for PARCEL 206 due then on September 1, 2018, would be $0.00.

On that November 18, 2017, pursuant to the same existing 2016 records of the Cook County Treasurer, the **"projected"** second installment tax bill for PARCEL 209, due then on September 1, 2018, would be:

$571.24.

On November 18, 2017, the **"projected"** second installment property tax bill for Loan #11147585, due then on September 1, 2018, would be $571.24.

That is exactly why Hansen had asked Byline's escrow department to manually re-run the escrow analysis to Loan #11147585.

INSTEAD, Exhibit 14 is Hansen's December 7, 2017, e-mail to me:

Mr. Barrett, they are asking for a copy of the letter you received from the County relative to the reduction in taxes via your appeal. Please either scan it to my e-mail or fax it to 312/460=3795.

Yes, I received it.

Then Kenig will forever fraudulently deny there was ever any reduction in the tax for PARCEL 206 and will forever fraudulently deny that our actual 2017 Assessment Appeal Number 0113329 for PARCEL 206 and continuous PARCEL 207 ever existed and was ever granted by the Cook County Assessor to forever fraudulently deny that the 2017 Assessed Value of PARCEL 206 was ever $29,019.

SEE: FACTS/FIX

Byline is not a Ma and Pa Grocery Store. Byline is a multi-billion-dollar bank with its own escrow department.

"they" did not need that October 7, 2017 letter from the Cook County Assessor to already know that the **"projected"** second installment property tax bill for Loan #11147585, due then on September 1, 2018, was $571.24 with the 2017 Assessed Value of PARCEL 206 being $29,019.

Exactly because of that December 7, 2017 e-mail, we already knew that something was already very wrong.

Exhibit 15 is Hansen's January 4, 2018, e-mail to me:

"Mr. Barrett, I apologize for not getting back to you. I am trying to get a positive answer on your request to have the escrow analysis recalculated based upon your positive protest of the tax amount.

However, I am being told that the recalculation will only be done once we get something official from the County as to the new amount of the taxes for 2017. This means that until we receive the 2nd installment tax bill, which would reflect the actual amount of the tax adjustment, we will not recalculate the escrow analysis. I am trying to meet with my boss today to review this with her, so I will get back to you today.

On January 4, 2018, the **"projected"** second installment property tax bill for Loan #11147585 was $571.24.

Pursuant to the actual provisions of Loan #11147585, after our February 16, 2018, payment of $3,127.00 to Byline, no further escrow payments could ever be, and never were, **"required"** of us by Byline.

INSTEAD, until Byline knew the exact amount of the 2nd installment for PARCEL 206 and PARCEL 209, pursuant to Byline's October 31, 2017, ANNUAL ESCROW DISCLOSURE STATEMENT Byline wanted $12,256.40 of our monies on Byline's balance sheet on August 18, 2018, one month before our Loans with Byline were to expire, to pay that **"projected"** 2nd installment property tax bill for Loan #11147585 of $571.24.

We would have to be abject morons to do so.

By that January 4, 2018 e-mail, it was already glaringly obvious to us that Byline had no intention of ever-renewing our two actual Loans with Byline and that Byline was already planning to cause the foreclosure of our actual Property at the time of renewal of those two Loans to seize our actual Property for vastly below its actual market value of $580,000.00

Accordingly, we would never even attempt to renew our actual Loans with Byline and, upon receipt of the tax refunds from the Cook County Treasurer, would refinance our actual Loans with Byline elsewhere.

We paid Byline $3,127.00 on January 16, 2018, to sufficiently fund our property tax escrow account for Loan #1114595 to pay the first installment property tax bill for PARCEL 206 and PARCEL 209 due on March 1, 2018, and to specifically protect that already REQUIRED LOW POINT BALANCE of that $3,275.08 to prevent Byline from causing the foreclosure of our actual Property.

Exhibit 16 is Hansen's January 26, 2018, e-mail to me again denying our request to have our monthly tax payments adjusted.

Pursuant to that e-mail, on January 26, 2018, the ENTIRE DEPARTMENTS of Byline already knew that the 2017 Assessed Value of PARCEL 206 was $29,019.

In the first week of February 2017, the State Equalizer was published. It increased from 2.8032 to 2.8627. The second installment property tax bill for Loan #11147585, due then on September 1, 2018, would still be less than $600.00 because PARCEL 206 is being reclassified as Class 2-12 to be assessed at 10% of market value.

Exhibit 17 and in the filed record is the 2017 Cook County Treasurer First Installment Property Tax Bill for PARCEL 206:

Classification 2-12

On February 13, 2018, Byline paid $ 10, 109.52 for PARCEL 206.

Exhibit 18 and in the filed record is the Cook County Treasurer First Installment Property Tax Bill for continuous PARCEL 207:

Classification 2-12

On February 13, 2018, Byline paid $ 1,606.85 for continuous PARCEL 207

Exhibits 17 and 18, as paid by Byline on that February 13, 2018, are the exact evidence that our 2017 Assessment Appeal Number 0113329 did exist and was granted by the Cook County Assessor and that the 2017 Assessed Value of PARCEL 206 was already $29,019 due to the change in classification for PARCEL 206.

AFTER Byline paid those Classification 2-12 Property Tax Bills for PARCEL 206 and continuous PARCEL 207 on February 13, 2018, Byline then engaged the services of Kenig to forever fraudulently deny that PARCEL 206 and continuous PARCEL 207 were ever correctly reclassified by the Cook County Assessor as

Classification 2-12 to be assessed at 10% of market value; to specifically forever fraudulently deny that PARCEL 206 was ever Class 2-12 to be assessed at 10% of market value; but was always Kenig's fraudulent misclassification of Classification 517 to be always be assessed at 25% of market value: to cause the criminal, fraudulent foreclosure of our actual Property:

SEE: FACTS/FIX

Because of those two suspicious e-mails, before making our February 16, 2018, payment to Byline, I called the Escrow Department of Byline to find out the balance in our property tax escrow account for Loan #11147585.

As corroborated in the filed record by Kenig, after Byline paid the first installment of property tax bills for PARCEL 206 and PARCEL 209, the property tax escrow balance account for Loan #1147585 was: $3,388.25.

Under the actual provisions of Loan #11147585, on February 16, 2018, we could have only paid Byline $600.00 in escrow payment for Loan #11147585 to pay the second installment property tax bill for PARCEL 206 and PARCEL 209 and still protect that REQUIRED LOW POINT BALANCE of $3,275.08 for Loan #11147585.

Instead, exactly because of those two suspicious e-mails, on February 16, 2018, we paid Byline $3,271.00 to specifically overfund the property tax escrow account for Loan #11147585 to prevent Byline from causing the foreclosure of our Property by protecting that REQUIRED LOW POINT BALANCE of that $3,275.08.

Pursuant to our actual 2017 Assessment Appeal Number 0113329 for PARCEL 206 and continuous PARCEL 207, as granted by the Cook County Assessor on November 18,

2017, Exhibit Group 19 are the six Certificates of Error for PARCEL 206 and continuous PARCEL 207 for the years 2014; 2015; and 2016 as granted by the Cook County Assessor on February 13, 2018, and as provided to us by Raila on February 27, 2018.

Specifically, the 2016 Certificate of Error for PARCEL 206:

RE: 15-21-301-206-0000

2016 CERTIFICATE OF ERROR NUMBER 00447952

CERTIFIED ON: FEBRUARY 13, 2018

CERTIFIED ASSESSED VALUE   24,881

ORIGINAL TAX AMOUNT   18,380.95

ADJUSTED AMOUNT   5,997.45

THE CLASS WAS INCORRECT BASED ON THE USE OF THE PROPERTY

That "PROPERTY" is Lot 1

On October 31, 2017, the 2017 Assessed value of PARCEL 206 was still: $63,025

On February 13, 2018, the 2016 Assessed value of PARCEL 206 is now: $24,881.

On October 31, 2017, the 2016 Total Tax for PARCEL 206 was $18,145.15

On February 13, 2018, the 2016 Total Tax for PARCEL 206 is now $5,997.45.

On October 31, 2017, the "aggregate" 2016 Total Tax for PARCEL 206 and PARCEL 209 was $19,850.95

On February 13, 2018, the "aggregate" 2016 Total Tax for PARCEL 206 and PARCEL 209 is now $7,266.95.

For us to receive those approximate $39,000.00 in property tax refunds, we had to evidence to the Cook County Treasurer that we had paid the real estate property tax bills for 2014, 2015, and 2016.

Accordingly, Exhibit 20 and in the filed record is my February 27, 2018, e-mail to Hansen:

HI MARK: MY C OF S FOR THE YEARS 2014, 2015, AND 2016 HAVE BEEN ACCEPTED BY THE COOK COUNTY TREASURER. FOR MYSELF TO RECEIVE THOSE SUBSTANTIAL REFUNDS, I NEED TO PROVE THAT BYLINE BANK PAID THE REAL ESTATE TAX BILLS PLEASE PROVIDE AT YOU EARLIEST CONVENIENCE

Hansen provided those documents for PARCEL 206 and continuous PARCEL 207; I lodged those PARCEL 206 and continuous PARCEL 207 documents with the Cook County Treasurer; Raila received those approximately $39,00.00 refunds; and we received those refunds minus Raila's fees.

By that May 8, 2018 letter, Kenig fraudulently denied those six Certificate of Errors for PARCEL 206 and continuous PARCEL 207 ever existed and fraudulently denied we ever received those refunds by fraudulently denying that our actual 2017 Assessment Appeal Number 0113329 for PARCEL 206 and continuous PARCEL 207 ever existed and was ever granted by the Cook County Assessor.

Memo: #11147585 P&I

Exhibit 21 and in the filed record is Byline's Loan Payment Notice for Note #11147585 as dated March 1, 2018:

Principal Balance	227,865.24
Payment Due Date	MAR 16, 2018

Your Payment Consists of

Principal	746.72
Interest	798.83
Escrow	1,671.45
Total Payment Due	3,271.00

Pursuant to the actual provisions of Note #11147585, and as would be admitted by Byline and evidenced by Kenig, there was no Escrow due Byline on March 16, 2018, and all that was due to Byline that on March 16, 2018 was $1,455.55 for Principal and Interest.

Ms. Todd called to inform us that the Cook County Treasurer had processed our documents for PARCEL 206 and continuous PARCEL 207 and that we could expect those property tax refunds in six weeks.

Exactly because of those two suspicious e-mails, at Exhibit 22 on March 14, 2018, we had already started the process of refinancing our actual two Loans with Byline elsewhere.

We would never risk even trying to renew our two actual Loans with Byline because of those two suspicious e-mails. We would pay substantial refinancing costs and accept higher interest rate loans to prevent Byline from causing the foreclosure of our actual Property at the time of renewal.

Also, exactly because of those two suspicious e-mails, Exhibit 23 and in the filed record is my March 16, 2018 e-mail to Hansen:

HI MARK:

Today am making my loan payment for Loan #11147585 with two checks marked P&I and Escrow. The check is for $1,455.55.

The Escrow check is for $400. I will continue to make Escrow payments of $400 each month.

The subject loan expires on September 16, 2018. As such, as of now, there is no current reason to re-cut the escrow payments for 2019.

Pursuant to the official Cook County records sought and provided to the Credit Department, at present, there is a SURPLUS in the real estate tax escrow account.

As such, for the April 16, 2018, payment for the subject loan, there will be no shortage, no late payment, and no late fees, only SURPLUS.

Even though under the actual provisions of Loan #11147585, after our February 16, 2018, payment of $3,271.00 by us to Byline, there were no further, and never were, any monthly escrow payments "**required**" of us by Byline, we specifically added $400 to the property tax escrow account for Loan #11147585 to protect the already REQUIRED LOW POINT BALANCE of that $3,275.08 to prevent Byline from causing the foreclosure of our actual Property.

It is the unilateral right of every Mortgagor to add monies to a real estate property escrow account, and our adding that $400 on March 16, 2018, could never be, and never was, any **"Event of Default"** declared by Byline under the actual provisions of Loan #11147585.

Exhibit 24, and in the filed record, is our March 16, 2018 check for $1,455.55 as specifically marked "Memo #11147585 P&I" and cashed by Byline on that March 18, 2018.

Exhibit 25, and in the filed record, is our March 16, 2018 check for $400.00 as specially marked "Memo #11147585 ESCROW" and cashed by Byline on that March 16, 2018.

After making those separate payments personally, the phone was already ringing as I walked in the door. It was Hansen screaming at me:

"Mr. Barrett, you cannot do that. If you do not give Byline all of its monies, Byline will never renew your Loans."

I told Hansen there was no shortage in the escrow account, only surplus, and that we were never going to renew our loans with Byline, and we had already started the process of refinancing our loans with Byline and just hung up the phone.

It does not require a leap of faith to understand that Hansen, the former courteous gentleman, had been ordered by Byline to have $12,256.40 of our money on Byline's balance sheet on August 18, 2018, at the time that Byline was already planning to cause the foreclosure of our actual Property.

Byline could not live without our $12,256.40 on its balance sheet when Byline would cause the foreclosure of our actual Property at the time of the renewals for our two Loans.

Robert Wilson Vice President Byline Bank

Exactly because Byline now knew that we were already planning to renew our Loans with Byline elsewhere, Exhibit 26 and in the filed record is Byline's fraudulently fabricated PAST DUE NOTICE for Note #11147585 dated March 26, 2018:

DEAR CUSTOMER -

WE AGAIN CALL YOUR ATTENTION TO THE NOTE PAST DUE AS DESCRIBED HEREIN.

PRINCIPAL BALANCE	226,409.69		
PAYMENT DUE DATE	MAR 16, 2018		
AMOUNT OF PAYMENT	2,832.56		
PRINCIPAL	746.72		
INTEREST	308.83		
LATE CHARGES	105.56		
ESCROW	1,671.45		
TOTAL PAST DUE	2,832.56		
Do the math:	March 1, 2018, Principal Balance	227,865.24	
	March 26, 2018, Principal Balance	226 409.69	
		1,455.55	

Byline fraudulently removed our entire March 16, 2018, payment of $1,455.55 to "P&I" from "Your Payment Consists of" to that fraudulently fabricated March 26, 2018 "Principal Balance" of that $226,409.69 to fraudulently deny that we had made that March 16, 2018 payment of that exact $1,455.55 to "P&I" to fraudulently fabricate a **"default"** that never existed to cause the criminal, fraudulent foreclosure of our actual Property.

Byline also fraudulently entered our March 16, 2018, "Escrow" payment of $400.00 as "Interest."

It does not require a leap of faith to understand that the person who made those fraudulent entries did not see those March 16, 2018, checks specifically marked "P&I" and "Escrow."

There never were any LATE CHARGES nor any PAST DUE AMOUNT for Note #11147585.

Exhibit 27 is Byline's fraudulently fabricated Loan Payment Notice for Note #11147585 as dated April 2, 2018.

Principal Balance	226,409.69
Payment Due Date	APR 16, 2018

Your Payment Consists of

Principal	675.70
Interest	779.85
Late Charges	105.56
Past Due Amount	2,727.00
Escrow	1,671.45
Total Payment Due	5,959.56

AGAIN, our entire March 16, 2018 payment of $1,455.55 to "P&I" was fraudulently entered into that April 2, 2018, Principal Balance of that $226,409.69; there never were any Late Charges, nor Past Due Amount; nor any Escrow due on April 16, 2018.

All that Byline was due on April 16, 2018, was $1,455.55 for Principal and Interest and not that fraudulently fabricated by Byline's Total Payment Due of that $5,959.56.

On April 5, 2018, 1 sent Hansen an e-mail entitled MISSING $1,455.55 and informed Hansen that we had paid Byline $1,455.55 for "P&I" on March 26, 2018 and that nothing was ever PAST DUE for Note #11147585:

NO RESPONSE

INSTEAD, Exhibit 28 is fraudulently fabricated by Byline PAST DUE NOTICE for Note #11147585 as dated April 15, 2018:

DEAR CUSTOMER:

YOUR PAYMENT IS NOW ONE MONTH PAST DUE

We were now in a fraudulently fabricated 30-day **"default"** that never existed.

PRINCIPAL BALANCE	226,409.69
PAYMENT DUE DATE	MAR 16, 2018
AMOUNT OF PAYMENT	2,832.56
PRINCIPAL	746.72

Frank J. Barrett

INTEREST	308.83
LATE CHARGES	105.56
ESCROW	1,671.56
TOTAL PAST DUE	2,832.56

Byline had cashed our March 16, 2018 payment of $1,455.55 to "P&I"; there never were any LATE CHARGES; there never was any ESCROW due; and none of that fraudulently fabricated by Byline's TOTAL PAST DUE of that $2,832,56 ever existed.

Exhibits 29 and 30 are our two April 16, 2018 checks specifically marked Principal and Interest and ESCROW. We again added $400.00 to ESCROW to protect the already REQUIRED LOW POINT BALANCE to prevent Byline from causing the foreclosure of our actual Property.

Exhibit 31 and in the filed record is the sham April 18, 2018 **"demand letter"** as evidenced by Wilson for Byline; and prepared by Kenig, which Wilson and Kenig and then collusive Robles will forever fraudulently deny ever existed.

The words **"escrow"** and **"taxes"** do not occur in that actual sham April 18, 2018 "demand letter" as prepared by Kenig:

Our office has been retained by Byline Bank (the "Bank") to initiate collection proceedings with respect to the following loans (the "Loans"):

B. Statement as to Default:

Prior to taking legal action, the Bank hereby notifies you that Loan #11147585 is in default as a result of the Borrower's failure to pay the March 16, 2018, monthly installment due and owing under Loan #11147585.

That was the exact criminal conspiracy of Byline and Wilson to cause the criminal, fraudulent foreclosure of our actual Property: fraudulently deny that we had made that March 16, 2018 payment of $1,455.55 to "P&I" to fraudulently fabricate that "default" that never existed in Loan #11147585:

The Bank hereby declares a default under Loan #11147245 as a result of the foregoing default under Loan #11147585.

Neither of those fraudulently fabricated by Byline and Wilson "defaults" ever existed.

C. Statement as to Amount Due:

As a result of the defaults outlined above, the Bank hereby accelerates all amounts due and owing under the Loans which are now due and payable".

Neither of those two fraudulently fabricated by Byline and Wilson "defaults outlined above" ever existed.

As of April 16, 2018, the total amount due and owing under the Loans was as follows:

LOAN #11147585		**LOAN #11147245**	
Principal:	$226,409.69	**Principal**	$181,874.13
Interest:	1,088.68	**Interest:**	(505.46)
Late Charges	105.56	**Late Charges**	0.00
Total Amount Due	$227,603.93	**Total Amount Due**	$182,379.59

AGAIN, our entire March 16, 2018 payment in the amount of $1,455.55 to "P&I" for Note #11147585 was removed by Byline from "Your Payment Consists of" to that April 16, 2018 Principal of that $226,409.69 for Byline and Wilson to fraudulently fabricate those two "defaults" that never existed.

By the admittance of Wilson for Byline, under the actual provisions of Loan #11147585, there never was any "Escrow" as any "amount due and owing" by us to Byline after our February 16, 2018 payment to Byline of $3.127.00.

AS EVIDENCED in the filed record by Kenig, on that April 18, 2018, the approximate balance in our property tax escrow account for Loan #11147585 was $5,800.00.

HOWEVER, Byline would never admit to any balance in our property tax escrow account for Loan #11147585 until AFTER Byline and Kenig had caused the criminal, fraudulent foreclosure of our actual Property, for obvious reasons.

If you have any questions, can call me or contact Robert Wilson at the Bank. Mr. Wilson's direct number is 773.890.3509.

WILSON

After Byline and Kenig had caused the criminal, fraudulent foreclosure of our actual Property, by sworn AFFIDAVIT, Wilson will brag that Wilson was responsible for the data entry of Loan #11147585:

WHAT A COINCIDENCE

KENIG

I called Kenig upon receipt of that actual sham April 18, 2018 **"demand letter"** as prepared by Kenig:

"Mr. Kenig, this is Frank Barrett. What the hell do you think you are doing?

"Mr. Barrett, I have been ordered by Byline Bank to foreclose on your property because you missed your March 16, 2018, payment of principal and interest."

"Really. Then why am I holding a copy of our March 16, 2018 check as specifically marked "P&I" in the amount of $1,455.55 as cashed by Byline Bank on that March 16, 2018?"

"What? Then why am I doing this?"

"You are doing this so Byline Bank can cause the fraudulent foreclosure of our Property and criminally seize our Property for vastly below its market value. And, as you already admitted, there is no escrow due. When the property taxes are paid, Byline owes us a refund."

"Mr. Barrett, if you are owed a refund, it will be safe with the Bank after we foreclose."

"Mr. Kenig, you are not foreclosing on anything. The exact reason there is no escrow due is that our home and the offices are classified by the Cook County Assessor as Class 2-12."

"Mr. Barrett, I cannot see how your home and the offices are Class 2-12."

"Mr. Kenig, I do not give a damn what you see. That is on the Assessor Website."

"Oh. Please send me a copy of that check."

Kenig was very sad that Kenig could not foreclose on our Property.

I sent Kenig a fax entitled CANCELLED CHECK and a copy of the Cook County Assessor's November 18, 2017, Final decision on our 2017 Assessment Appeal Number 0113329 for PARCEL 206: Class 2-12.

This matter should have been over. Wilson for Byline had admitted that there was never any Escrow as any "amount due and owing under the Loans" after our February 16, 2018 payment of $3,127.00 to Byline, and Kenig had a copy of our March 16, 2018 check as payment to "P&I" as cashed by Byline on that March 16, 2018.

INSTEAD, Exhibit 32 is fraudulently fabricated by Byline Loan Payment Notice for Note #11147585 as dated May 1, 2018:

Principal Balance   225,662.97
Payment Due Date   MAY 16, 2018

Your Payment Consists of

Principal	703.34
Interest	752.21
Late Charges	251.12
Past Due Amount	4,398.45
Escrow	1,671.45
Total Payment Due	7,776.57

For the reasons stated and evidenced, there never were any "Late Charges" of $251.12; never were any "Past Due Amount" of $4,398.45; and never any "Escrow" due; and never any "Total Payment Due" of that fraudulently fabricated by Byline $7,776.57 due on May 16, 2018, for Note #11147585.

All that was due and owing by us to Byline on May 1, 2018, was $1,455.55 for Principal and Interest.

Exhibit 33 is Kenig's May 8, 2018 letter by which Kenig forever fraudulently denied that sham actual April 18, 2018 **"demand letter"** as prepared by Kenig ever existed:

Part of the collateral for the Loan is the real property and improvements located at 1600 Westchester Boulevard, Westchester, IL (the "Property"). According to the Bank's loan policies from Chicago Title, the PIN Nos. for the Property are 15-21-301=206 and 15-21-301-209.

Kenig's fraudulently fabricated "Property" is only PARCEL 206, which use for property taxation purposes is our actual single-story Westchester Medical Center, 1600, and PARCEL 209, which for use for property tax purposes is our detached residential garage.

The last full-year tax bill for the Property was 2016 at which time the aggregate real estate taxes for both PIN Nos. was $19,650.45.

Pursuant to the records of the Cook County Assessor, as of February 13, 2018, the "aggregate" 2016 property taxes for PARCEL 206 and PARCEL 209 was exactly $7,266.95 because of the change in classification of PARCEL 206 to Classification 2-12 to be assessed at 10% of market value.

Figuring a modest 5.0% increase for the 2017 real estate taxes ($982.52), the estimated 2017 real estate taxes for the Property would be $20, 632.98.

AS EVIDENCED by Kenig in the filed record for that June 19, 2019 hearing, as demanded by Byline and Kenig for the fraudulent procurement of that Receivership, the actual 2017 Total Taxes for PARCEL 206 and PARCEL 209 were $7,170.80 exactly because of the change in classification of PARCEL 206 to Class 212 to be assessed at 10% of market value.

Dividing that estimate by 12 equals a monthly tax escrow payment of $1,719.41. However, as you know, the current monthly tax escrow for Loan #11147585 is $1,671.45.

As Kenig already knew, as admitted by Wilson for Byline in that actual sham April 18, 2018 **"demand letter"** as prepared by Kenig, pursuant to the actual provisions of Loan #11147585 after our February 16, 2018 payment of $3,127.00 to Byline, no further monthly escrow payments were "required," and never could be, "required" of us by Byline.

"Notwithstanding, you have unilaterally decided to pay $400.00 a month towards the required real estate tax escrow, ...

AGAIN, as admitted by Wilson for Byline in that actual sham April 18, 2018 "demand letter" as prepared by Kenig, pursuant to the actual provisions of Loan #11147585, no further monthly escrow payments were ever "required," and never could be "required" of us by Byline after our February 16, 2018 payment of $3,127.00 to Byline **..... based on the Certificate of Error that you filed with the Cook County Assessor seeking to change the Property's classification from 517 (one-story commercial building) to 2-12 (mixed-use commercial/residential building).**

Kenig will admit that we filed a Certificate of Error with the Cook County Assessor but will forever fraudulently deny that we ever filed our actual 2017 Assessment Appeal Number 0113329 for PARCEL 206 and PARCEL 207 and that our actual 2017 Assessment Appeal Number 0113329 was ever granted by the Cook County Assessor to forever fraudulently deny that PARCEL 206 was ever reclassified as Class 212 to be assessed at 10% of market value but was always Kenig's fraudulently misclassified Class 517 to be assessed at 25% of market value:

SEE: FACTS/FIX

INSTEAD, Kenig's fraudulently fabricated **"Property"** is only PARCEL 206, which for property taxation purposes is our actual single-story Westchester Medical Center, 1600, and PARCEL 209, which for property taxation purposes is our actual detached residential garage.

Kenig's fraudulently fabricated **"Certificate of Error"** for PARCEL 206 and PARCEL 209 never existed.

Kenig has fraudulently denied that our actual 2017 Assessment Appeal Number 0113329 for PARCEL 206 and continuous PARCEL 207 ever even existed and was ever granted by the Cook County Assessor,

Although you claim in your e-mails to me that "1600 is the Westchester Medical Center office building [with PIN Nos. 15-21-301-206 and 15-21-301-2091 and your personal residence [with PIN No. 15-21301-207], ...

No such fraudulently fabricated by Kenig "e-mails" ever existed.

Pursuant to my actual "e-mail":

1600-1606 is ONE 4,000-square-foot building with less than six units: MIXED USE.

PIN 15-21-301-209 is a six-car garage in the parking lot of 1600.

Then after Kenig having fraudulently fabricated that "e-mail" that never existed:

**"I fail to see the basis for your conclusion that
"1600-1606 is ONE mixed-use building."**

**TWO FRAUDULENTLY FABRICATED,
PHYSICALLY IMPOSSIBLE SEPARATE BUILDINGS**

SEE: FACTS/FIX

SEE 1600-1606 Westchester Boulevard

First, Kenig and then collusive Robles will forever fraudulently deny that

"1600-1606 is ONE mixed-use building."

But always fraudulently claimed that our actual totally attached custom-built 1600-1606 always located on Lot 1, was always Kenig's:

**TWO FRAUDULENTLY FABRICATED,
PHYSICALLY IMPOSSIBLE TWO SEPARATE BUILDINGS**

SEE: FACTS/FIX

SEE: 1600-1606 Westchester Boulevard

As I tried to explain to you over the phone, despite your optimism that the Assessor will grant your Certificate of Error and thereby lower the assessed value of the Property, resulting in a lower tax bill.

No such fraudulently fabricated by Kenig conversation ever occurred.

I had informed Kenig in that actual phone call that the Cook County Assessor had already granted our Certificate of Error on its Website and had faxed Kenig the evidence of such.

On February 13, 2018, Byline had already paid the Cook County Treasurer Classification 2-12 First Installment Property Tax Bills for PARCEL 206 and continuous PARCEL

207 as the exact evidence that our actual 2017 Assessment Appeal Number 0113329 did exist, had already been granted by the Cook County Assessor; and that the 2017 Assessed Value of PARCEL 206 was already $29,019 due to the change in classification of PARCEL 2-12.

.... the basis of the Bank's calculation of the monthly escrow payment for 2018 is the estimated amount of the 2017 real estate taxes. Until that estimated amount is verified to be different than as estimated by the Bank (which will not occur until the 2nd installment of the 2017 real estate taxes are assessed),...

On October 31, 2017, with PARCEL 206 still being Class 517 with a 2016 Assessed value of $63,025, the **"projected"** 2nd installment property tax bill for Loan #1114758 was that $8,981.32.

On November 18, 2017, with PIN 206 being Class 2-12 with a 2017 Assessed Value of $29,019, the "projected" 2nd installment property tax bill for Loan #11147585 was $571.24.

That is exactly why, on November 24, 2017, that Hansen had asked Byline's escrow department to re-cut the escrow analysis for Loan #11147585.

Byline did not have wait until the 2nd installment property tax bill for PARCEL 206 was issued to know that as of November 18, 2017, the "projected" 2nd property tax bill for PARCEL 206 would be different than that "projected" by Byline on October 31, 2017.

As such, Kenig forever fraudulently denies that as of November 18, 2018 the Cook County Assessor Website, the 2017 Assessed Value of PARCEL 206 was already $29,019.

... you do not have the right to unilaterally decide to adjust the monthly escrow amount.

Wilson for Byline had already admitted that after our February 16, 2018, payment of $3,127.00 to Byline, no further monthly escrow payments were "required" of us by Byline under the actual provisions of Loan #11147585.

Adding $400.00 to the property tax escrow account of Loan #11147585 on March 16, 2018, is the unilateral right of every Mortgagor and was never any "Event of Default" as ever declared by Byline.

For this reason, the Bank issued a demand letter to you dated April 18, 2018, declaring the Loan to be in default and accelerating all sums due and payable under the Loan.

No such fraudulently fabricated by Kenig **"reason"** ever existed.

Byline and Wilson had Kenig issue that actual sham April 18, 2018 **"demand letter"** by fraudulently fabricating that we failed to make our March 16, 2018 payment of $1,455.55

for Principal and Interest to cause the criminal, fraudulent accelerated foreclosure of our actual Property with those two fraudulently fabricated by Byline and Wilson **"defaults"** that never existed.

No such now fraudulently fabricated by Kenig **"default"** ever existed in our real estate property tax escrow account for Note $11147585 ever existed.

No such fraudulently fabricated April 18, 2018, "demand letter" ever existed.

The words **"escrow"** and **"tax"** do not occur in that actual sham April 18, 2018, "demand letter," as prepared by Kenig.

Wilson for Byline had already admitted in that actual sham April 18, 2018 "demand letter" as prepared by Kenig that no Escrow was ever any "sums due and owing under the Loan" of us to Byline after our February 16, 2018 payment of $3,127.00 to Byline. So Kenig just simply fraudulently fabricated another entire April 18, 2018 "demand letter" that never existed to fraudulently fabricate another "default" in our property tax escrow account for Loan #11147585 that never could have existed for Byline and Kenig to cause the criminal, fraudulent foreclosure of our actual Property with Kenig's fraudulent misclassification of PARCEL 206 as Class 517 to be assessed at 25% of market value:

SEE: FACTS/FIX

In the meantime, despite the continuing default under the Loan, so long as the monthly principal and interest payments of $1,455.55 continue to be paid with the monthly tax escrow amount of $400.00 (which the Bank continues to dispute as outlined above), the Bank has decided at this time to delay exercising its rights and remedies under the Loan as a result of the foregoing default.

That fraudulently fabricated by Kenig's "foregoing default" never existed.

If a **"default"** did exist, we had to pay Kenig's legal fees.

If a **"default"** did not exist, Byline had to pay Kenig's legal fees.

Byline and Kenig wanted us to continue to pay $400.00 in monthly escrow payments and thereby admit we were in Kenig's fraudulently fabricated "default" that never existed.

"Furthermore, if there is a shortfall in the real estate tax escrow when the 2nd installment tax bill is issued, you will have five (5) days to deposit additional funds in tax escrow to enable the Bank to pay the 2nd installment tax bill. Your failure to do so will result in another event of default."

Byline never declared any **"event of default"** in our real estate property tax escrow account for Loan #11147585.

That was Kenig's **"interpretation"** of the actual provisions of Loan #11147585.

Exactly because of those two suspicious e-mails, on February 16, 2018; March 16, 2018; and April 16, 2018 we had specifically already overfunded the real estate property tax escrow account for Loan #11147585 to protect the REQUIRED LOW POINT BALANCE to ensure exactly that there would never be any "shortfall" when the 2nd installment property tax bill for PARCEL 206 and PARCEL 209 was issued by the Cook County Treasurer.

Most importantly, the Loan and Loan No. 11147245 (collectively, the "Loans") have a stated maturity date of September 21, 2018. The Bank will not be extending the stated maturity date of the Loans and will not be refinancing them either.

Exactly because of those two suspicious e-mails, we had no intention of ever-renewing our actual Loans with Byline, and on March 14, 2018, we had already started the process of refinancing our actual Loans with Byline elsewhere.

cc. Robert Wilson (via electronic mail only)

The **"Bank"** is Wilson.

That is the exact same Wilson who had admitted in that actual sham April 18, 2018, "demand letter" as prepared by Kenig that there was never any "default" in our real estate property tax escrow account for Loan #11147585.

Exhibit 34, as fraudulently fabricated by Byline, is the PAST DUE NOTICE for Note #11147585 as dated May 15, 2018:

YOUR PAYMENT IS NOW TWO MONTHS PAST DUE

NONE of our PAYMENTS were ever PAST DUE.

For the reasons stated and evidenced, none of that fraudulently fabricated by Byline's TOTAL PAST DUE of that $4,649.57 ever existed.

Exhibit 35 a is our May 16, 2018, payment of $1,455.55 to Byline for Principal and Interest.

Exactly because on April 18, 2018, Wilson had admitted that no Escrow was due May 16, 2018, we ceased overfunding our real estate property tax escrow account for Notre #11147585.

Exhibit 36 is the fraudulently fabricated Byline Loan Payment Notice for Note #11147585 dated June 2, 2018:

For the reasons stated and evidenced, all that was due and owing of us by Byline on June 16, 2018, was $1,455.55 for Principal and Interest and not that fraudulently fabricated by Byline's Total Payment Due of that $9,593.58.

Exhibit 37 is our June 16, 2018, check paid to Byline for $1,455.55 for Principal and Interest.

Exhibit 38 is the fraudulently fabricated by Byline PAST DUE NOTICE for Note #11147585 as dated June 17, 2018:

YOUR PAYMENT IS NOW TWO MONTHS PAST DUE

None of our PAYMENTS were ever PAST DUE

For the reasons stated and evidenced, none of that fraudulently fabricated by Byline's TOTAL PAST DUE of that $9,593.58 ever existed.

On June 20, 2018, we paid First Secure Bank & Trust Company $1,000 for due diligence to refinance Loan #11147585. Wintrust would refinance Loan #11147245 based on that due diligence.

Exhibit 39, as fraudulently fabricated by Byline, is the Loan Payment Notice for Note #11147585 as dated July 2, 2018:

For the reasons stated and evidenced, all that was due and owing to Byline by us on July 16, 2018, was $1,455.55 for Principal and Interest and not that fraudulently fabricated by Byline's Total Payment Due of that $11,410.59.

Exhibit 40 is Kenig's July 3, 2018, letter to the Attorney Registration and Disciplinary Commission:

"The dispute with Mr. Barrett involves Loan No. 11147585, which requires monthly principal and interest payments in the amount of $1,455.55 along with a monthly tax escrow payment in the amount of $1,671.45 which is based on the estimated 2017 real estate taxes for the Property of $29,057.40. The real estate taxes for the Property in 2016 were $19,650.45."

As admitted by Wilson for Byline in that actual sham April 18, 2018 demand letter," as prepared by Kenig, Kenig's fraudulently fabricated "dispute" never existed.

Based on the foregoing, the monthly payment on Loan No. 11147585 is $3.127.00 ($1,455.55 + $16,71.45), which is due payable on the 16th day of each month. On March

16, 2018, instead of paying the Bank the required monthly installment of $3,127.00, Mr. Barrett paid the Bank $1,855.55, representing $1,455.55 for principal and interest and a tax escrow payment of $400.00.

The exact criminal conspiracy to defraud of Byline and Wilson in that actual sham April 18, 2018 demand letter" as prepared by Kenig was that we had failed to make that exact March 16, 2018 payment of that $1,455.00 to principal and interest to fraudulently fabricate those two "defaults" that never existed to cause the criminal accelerated fraudulent foreclosure of our actual Property.

Kenig just simply admitted such.

Mr. Barrett advised the Bank that because he had filed a real estate tax appeal with the Cook County Assessor and because he was convinced that the appeal would be granted, Mr. Barrett unilaterally decided what the monthly tax escrow should be based upon the outcome of the appeal.

Kenig will admit that we filed an appeal with the Cook County Assessor but will forever fraudulently deny that we filed any appeal for PARCEL 206 and continuous PARCEL 207 to forever fraudulently deny we ever advised Byline of the FINAL decision of the Cook County Assessor on that November 18, 2017, to forever fraudulently deny the 2017 Assessed Value of PARCEL 206 was ever $29,019:

As a result of Mr. Barrett's failure to pay the required monthly installment under Loan No. 11147585, the Bank requested that I issue a demand letter ("the Demand Letter) to the borrowers. I did so on April 18, 2018. A copy of the Demand Letter is enclosed.

Byline and Wilson had requested that Kenig issue that sham April 18, 2018 **"demand letter"** because we had failed to make our March 16, 2018 payment of $1,455.55 to Principal and Interest to fraudulently fabricate those two **"defaults"** that never existed to cause the criminal accelerated fraudulent foreclosure of our actual Property.

Again, Kenig had just admitted such.

The words **"escrow"** and **"taxes"** never occurred in that actual sham on April 18, 2018, **"demand letter,"** as prepared by Kenig.

So on May 8, 2018, Kenig had simply fraudulently fabricated an entire April 18, 2018 **"demand letter"** that never existed to fraudulently fabricate another **"default"** that could never have existed in our real estate property tax escrow account for Loan #11147585 for Byline and Kenig to cause the criminal, fraudulent foreclosure of our actual Property with Kenig's fraudulent misclassification of PARCEL 206 as Classification 517 to be assessed at 25% of market value:

SEE: FACTS/FIX

"The bottom line here is that Mr. Barrett has defaulted under the terms of the Loans .....

The actual **"bottom line here"** is that Kenig's fraudulently fabricated "default" in our real estate property tax escrow account for Note #111247585 never existed, as admitted by Wilson for Byline in that actual sham April 18, 2018 "demand letter" as prepared by Kenig.

On that same July 3, 2018, the Cook County Treasurer issued and provided to Byline the Classification 212 Second Property Tax Bill for PARCEL 206, already Exhibit 3 already attached herein:

As stated, first Byline and Kenig and then a collusive Robles will forever fraudulently deny that PARCEL 206 was ever Classification 2-12 to be assessed at 10% of market value but was always Kenig' fraudulent misclassification of Classification 517 to be assessed at 25% of market value; to forever fraudulently deny that the 2017 Assessed Value of PARCEL 206 was $29,019 but was always a fraudulently fabricated $72,547; to forever fraudulently deny that the 2017 Total Tax of PARCEL 206 was ever $6,643.29 but was always a fraudulently fabricated $19,836.25; to forever fraudulently deny that Byline and Kenig had caused the fraudulent foreclosure of our actual Property with Kenig's forever fraudulent misclassification of PARCEL 206 always being Classification 517 to be assessed at 25% of market value:

SEE: FACTS/FIX

Exhibit 41 is the Cook County Treasurer Classification 2-12 Second Installment Property Tax Bill for continuous PARCEL 207 as paid by Byline on July 13, 2018.

That is the exact 2017 Classification 2-12 property tax bill for continuous PARCEL 207 that Kenig had already fraudulently denied ever existed on May 8, 2018.

Exhibit 42 is the Cook County Treasurer 2017 Second Installment Property Tax Bill for PARCEL 209, in that amount of $566.72 paid by Byline on July 13,2018.

That is the $566.72 property tax bill that on January 4, 2018 that Byline wanted $12,256.40 of our money on Byline's balance sheet on August 18, 2018 when Byline planned to cause the foreclosure of our actual Property.

On that July 13, 2018 we were entitled to and received a refund in the amount of $3,466.33 for PARCEL 206 from the Cook County Treasurer because the Cook County Assessor had correctly reclassified PARCEL 206 as Class 2-12.

Exhibit 43 is our July 14, 2018 check in the amount of $1,455.55 to Byline for Principal and Interest. Exhibit 44 is Byline's fraudulently fabricated PAST DUE NOTICE for Note #11147585 as dated July 15,2018:

YOUR PAYMENT IS NOW THREE MONTHS PAST DUE

None of our **PAYMENTS** were ever any **PAST DUE**

For the reasons stated and evidenced, none of that fraudulently fabricated by Byline TOTAL PAST DUE of that $8,283,59 ever existed.

Exhibit 45 is the fraudulently fabricated by Byline Loan Payment Notice for Note #11147585 as dated August 1, 2018:

For the reasons stated and evidenced, all that was due and owing by us to on August 16, 2018 to Byline was $1,455.55 for Principal and Interest and not that fraudulently fabricated by Byline Total Payment Due of that $13,227.60.

Exhibit 46 is our August 16, 2018 check to Byline in the amount of $1,455.55 for Principal and Interest.

Pursuant to Byline's actual records, no Payments of ours was ever LATE: none of our monies was ever any PAST DUE AMOUNT: and we were never in any DEFAULT under the actual provisions of our actual Loans with Byline: NEVER.

AS EVIDENCED by Kenig with Byline's actual computer generated records and with PARCEL 206 being correctly reclassified bt the Cook County Assessor as Class 2-12 to be assessed at 10% of market value the actual PAYOFF for Loan #11157585 due on September 21, 2018 was:

Principal Balance	$224,316.64
Interest	897.26
Escrow	(5,117.25)
Total Payout	$217,989.65

Exactly because of the significant reduction in the 2017 real estate property taxes for PARCEL 206, the guaranteed rental income alone of our totally attached custom built Westchester Medical Center was sufficient to pay the principal; interest; real estate taxes; and insurance for both new Loans to be refinanced.

Accordingly, on August 20, 2018 by e-mail we were formally approved by First Secure Bank & Trust to refinance Loan #11147585 subject to what was actually owed Byline; mandatory appraisals; customary closing costs; and a simultaneous closing for Wintrust to refinance Loan #11147245.

First Secure also provided a list of approved appraisers to choose from.

I called Kenig and demanded actual PAYOFF STATEMENTS for both Loans. Kenig stated that we had missed monthly payments; that we were in default; and, over and over again, we had to pay Kenig's legal fees because we were in Kenig's fraudulently fabricated "default" that never existed.

Exhibits 47 and 48 are those PAYOFF STATEMENTS as prepared for Wilson and provided by Kenig and dated August 27, 2018:

Loan #11147585		Loan #11147245	
Principal Balance	$224,315.73	Principal Balance	$179.454.14
Interest	2,673.91	Interest	(399.33)
Late Fees	545.42	Late Fees	0.00
Legal Fee	3,278.03	Legal Fee	3,207.03
File Closing Fee	200.00	File Closing Fee	200.00
TOTAL PAYOFF	$231,022.09	TOTAL PAYOFF	$182,461.84

The actual Interest due on September 21, 2018 for Loan #11147585 was $897.26 and not that fraudulently fabricated by Byline $2,673.91.

There never were any "Late Fees" for Loan #11147585.

Byline and Wilson and Kenig were demanding that we pay Kenig's "Legal Fees" of $6,494.06 for Kenig fraudulently fabricating that entire April 18, 2018 "demand letter" that never existed to fraudulently fabricate that "default" that never existed in our actual real estate property tax escrow account for Loan #11147585 for Byline and Kenig to cause the criminal fraudulent foreclosure of our actual Property with Kenig's forever fraudulent misclassification of PARCEL 206 always being Class 517 to be assessed at 25% of market value.

As admitted by Byline, there was never any PAST DUE AMOUNT nor ever any "Escrow" due on September 21, 2018 for Loan #11147585.

As admitted by Byline, there was never any as fraudulently fabricated by Kenig "default" in our actual real estate property tax escrow account for Loan #11147585.

As evidenced in the record by Kenig after Byline and Kenig had caused the criminal fraudulent foreclosure of our actual Property, on that August 27, 2018 there was a balance of at least $5,117.25 in our property tax escrow account for Loan #11147585; and a balance of at least $1,800.00 in our property tax escrow account for Loan #11147245.

If Byline would have provided actual PAYOFF STATEMENTs for Loan #11147585 and Loan #111472345 with the actual Interest; without fraudulently fabricated "Late Fees";

without Kenig's criminal "Legal Fees"; and with credit for the balances in our actual real estate property tax escrow accounts, we would have already refinanced our actual Loans with Byline elsewhere and the criminal fraudulent foreclosure of our actual Property by Byline and Kenig would never have occurred.

INSTEAD, Exhibit 49, with PARCEL 206 being Kenig's forever fraudulent misclassification of PARCEL 206 always being Class 517 to be assessed at 25% of market value, is Byline's fraudulently fabricated Loan Payment Notice for Note #11147585 as dated September 6, 2018:

Principal Balance	224,315.73
Payment Due Date	SEP 21, 2018

Your Payment Consists of

Principal	$222,219.64
Interest	887.26
Late Charges	545.42
Past Due Amount	11,084.25
Escrow	1,671.45
Total Payment Due	$236,418.02

On April 18, 2018 Byline and Wilson had fraudulently fabricated those two **"defaults"** that never existed to cause the criminal fraudulent accelerated foreclosure of our actual Property;

When that failed, on May 8, 2018 Kenig just simply fraudulently fabricated an entire April 18, 2018 **"demand letter"** that never existed; to fraudulently fabricate another "default" that never existed; for Byline and Kenig to cause the criminal fraudulent foreclosure of our actual Property; with Kenig's forever fraudulent misclassification of PARCEL 206 always being Class 517 to be assessed at 25% of market value.

On July 15, 2018 Byline fraudulently fabricated "YOUR PAYMENT IS NOW THREE MONTHS PAST DUE" that never existed;

Now on September 6, 2018 Byline fraudulently fabricated "Late Charges" of $545.32 that never existed; fraudulently fabricated "Past Due Amount" of $11,084.25 that never existed; fraudulently fabricated "Escrow" of $1,671.45" that was never due on September 21, 2018; to fraudulently fabricate that "Total Payment Due" of that $236,418.02 that never existed.

In addition, first Byline and Kenig and then a now collusive Robles were demanding that we pay Kenig's criminal "Legal Fees" of $6496.06 for Kenig fraudulently fabricating all of the foregoing with Kenig's forever fraudulent misclassification of PARCEL 206 always being Class 517 to be assessed at 25% of market value.

AS EVIDENCED in the filed record, first Byline and Kenig and then a now collusive Robles were demanding a PAYOFF for Note #11147585 on that September 21, 2018 of:

$242,388.08

Those fraudulently fabricated three **"defaults"** that never existed; that fraudulently fabricated YOUR PAYMENT IS NOW THREE MONTHS PAST DUE that never existed; those fraudulently fabricated "Late Fees" that never existed; that fraudulently fabricated "Past Due Amount" that never existed; that fraudulently fabricated "Escrow" that was never due on September 21, 2018 that never existed; that fraudulently fabricated Total Payment Due" that never existed; and Kenig's criminal "Legal Fees" for fraudulently fabricating the foregoing with Kenig's forever fraudulent misclassification that PARCEL 206 was always Class 517 to be assessed at 25% of market value fraudulently preventing us from refinancing our actual Loan with Byline elsewhere.

We could not, did not, and would never pay the criminal extortion of that:

$242,388.08

On that September 6, 2018 my estimate of the actual balance in our property tax escrow account for Loan #11147585 was: $5,300.00, but we could not prove that.

Accordingly, our Attorney served on Kenig a QWR letter for Byline's actual records for Loan #11147585.

Kenig's answer was: N/A.

Byline's actual records would have exactly evidenced that Byline and Wilson and then Kenig had criminally conspired for parts of seven months to cause the fraudulent foreclosure of our actual Property so Byline could criminally seize our actual Property for vastly below its actual market value of $580,000.00.

18 CH 13221

Byline and Kenig having fraudulently prevented us from refinancing our actual Loans with Byline elsewhere with Kenig's forever fraudulent misclassification of PARCEL 206 always being Class 517 to be assessed at 25% of market value, on October 23, 2108 Kenig filed Byline's fraudulent COMPLAINT FOR FORECLOSURE AND OTHER RELIEF for Loan #11147585.

On that October 23, 2018 the outstanding balance on our two actual Loans with Byline was approximately $400.00.00.

Kenig will admit that on that same October 23, 2018 that the actual market value of our actual Property was $580,000.00.

Then Kenig will forever fraudulently deny that the actual market value of our actual Property was ever $580,000.00 to forever fraudulently deny that Byline and Kenig had caused the criminal fraudulent foreclosure of our actual Property for Byline to criminally seize our actual Property for vastly below its actual market value of that $580,000.00.

That October 23, 2018 COMPLAINT was never heard.

At the exact same time that Kenig was preparing Kenig's fraudulently fabricated physically impossible frauds upon the court, which could never have physically existed, to now forever fraudulently deny that PARCEL 206 was ever Class 2-12 to be assessed at 10% of market value but was always Kenig's misclassification of Class 517 to be assessed at 25% of market value to forever fraudulently deny that Byline and Kenig had caused the criminal fraudulent of our actual Property, Exhibits 50 and 51 are the Cook County Treasurer First Installment Property Tax Bills for LOT 1 for PARCEL 206 and continuous PARCEL 207:

Classification 2-12

Those are the Cook County Treasurer Classification 2-12 property tax bills for LOT 1 and for PARCEL 206 and continuous PARCEL 207 that Kenig had already fraudulently denied ever existed by Kenig's May 8, 2018 letter in which Kenig had already fraudulently denied that our actual 2017 Assessment Appeal Number 0113329 for PARCEL 206 and continuous PARCEL ever existed and was ever granted by the Cook County Assessor for LOT 1.

At Byline's fraudulent AMENDED COMPLAINT FOR FORECLOSURE AND OTHER RELIEF:

COUNT 1

(Foreclosure of Mortgage on 1600 Westchester Boulevard, Westchester, Illinois 60154)

2. Attached hereto as <u>Exhibit A</u> is a copy of the mortgage dated March 16, 2005 and recorded on March 25, 2005 (the "Mortgage).

Exhibit 52 is the first page of **<u>Exhibit A:</u>**

LOT 1 EXCEPT THE SOUTH 34.23 FEET .....

PIN No. 15-21-301-206-0000

COOK COUNTY PARCEL NUMBERS ARE NOT LOT NUMBERS

COUNT 2

(Foreclosure of Mortgage on 1606 Westchester Boulevard, Westchester, Illinois 60154)

2. Attached hereto as <u>Exhibit G</u> is a copy of the mortgage dated February 16, 2005 and recorded on February 25, 2005 (the "Mortgage").

Exhibit 53 is the first page of that **<u>Exhibit G:</u>**

THE SOUTH 34.23 FEET OF LOT 1 .....

PIN No. 15-21-301-207-0000

COOK COUNTY PARCEL NUMBERS ARE NOT LOT NUMBERS

Then Kenig's forever fraud upon the court, which will then become the FIX of then absolutely clueless Robles on June 19, 2019, is that LOT 1 never existed.

Kenig exactly evidenced Kenig's fraudulently fabricated physically impossible frauds upon the court with the actual genuine material legal descriptions of our actual **"Mortgages"** with Byline even before Kenig committed Kenig's fraudulently fabricated physically impossible frauds upon the court.

At Page 3 of that fraudulent AMENDED COMPLAINT for Note #11147585:

J. Statement as to default and amount owed:

The Note is in default by reason of non-payment of the sums due and owing at maturity. As of September 25, 2018, the indebtedness had not been paid and the following sums (excluding default interest and legal fees and costs) remaining due and owing under the Note and the Mortgage:

Principal Balance Due	**$224,315.73**
Interest	**3,299.31**
Late Charges	**545.42**
Escrow Balance	**(5,117.25)**
Total Due	**$223,043.21**

The actual Interest due on September 21, 2018 was $897.26 and not that fraudulently fabricated by Byline $3,299.31

There were never any fraudulently fabricated by Byline "Late Charges" for Loan #11147585.

There was never any fraudulently fabricated by Byline PAST DUE AMOUNT nor any fraudulently fabricated by Byline Escrow due on September 21, 2018 for Loan #11147585.

There was never any as fraudulently fabricated by Kenig **"default"** in our actual real estate property tax escrow account for Loan #11147585.

Kenig exactly evidenced that Byline and Kenig had caused the criminal fraudulent foreclosure of our actual Property by fraudulently preventing us from refinancing our actual Loans with Byline elsewhere with Kenig's forever fraudulent misclassification of PARCEL 206 always being Class 517 to be assessed at 25% of market value.

Kenig having already evidenced Kenig's fraudulently fabricated physically impossible frauds upon the court with the actual genuine material legal descriptions of our actual **"Mortgages"** with Byline before Kenig even committed Kenig's fraudulently fabricated physically impossible frauds upon the court; and already having evidenced that Byline and Kenig had caused the criminal foreclosure of our actual Property by Kenig forever fraudulently misclassifying PARCEL 206 as always being Class 517 to be assessed at 25% of market value, Kenig then filed Byline's MOTION FOR THE APPOINTMENT OF A RECEIVER to further fraudulently prevent us from ever refinancing our actual Loans with Byline elsewhere.

Exhibit 54 attached to that MOTION as Exhibit 1 is the sworn AFFIDAVIT OF ROBERT WILSON as an authorized agent of Byline for Note #11147585:

10. Attached hereto as Exhibit A is a computer-generated payoff screen from the Bank's computer system showing that as of September 25, 2018, the following sums (excluding default interest and amounts advanced by Bank) were due and owing under the Note and Mortgage:

Principal Balance Due	**$224,315.73**
Interest	**3,299.31**
Late Charges	**545.42**
Escrow Balance	**(5,117.25)**
Total Due	**$223, 043.21**

The actual Interest due on September 21, 2018 was $897.26 and not that fraudulently fabricated by Byline $3,299.31.

There were never any '(Late Charges" for Loan #11147585.

There was never and as fraudulently fabricated "Past Due Amount" nor any as fraudulently fabricated by Byline "Escrow" ever due on September 21, 2018.

Kenig's fraudulently fabricated "default" in our actual real estate property tax escrow account for Loan #11147585 never existed.

AGAIN, Kenig exactly evidenced that Byline and Kenig had caused the fraudulent criminal foreclosure of our actual Property by fraudulently preventing us from refinancing our actual Loans with Byline elsewhere with Kenig's forever fraudulent misclassification of PARCEL 206 always being Class 517 to be assessed at 25% of market value:

SEE: FACTS/FIX

Exactly because of Kenig's May 8, 2018 letter, at our DEFENDANTS' RESPONSE TO PLAINTIFF'S MOTION FOR RECEIVERSHIP is my sworn AFFIDAVIT:

My residence and the offices ate contained in 1 building located on:

Lot 1 in George F. Nixon & Company's Central Addition to Westchester, being a Subdivision ....

Exactly because of Kenig's May 8, 2018 letter, for that hearing as demanded by Byline our Exhibit 1, which is Exhibit 1 herein, was the actual Plat of Survey and the actual Warranty Deed with the actual legal description of our actual Property.

Our entire actual single-story custom built totally attached 1600-1606 has always been located entirely on that 100 foot wide:

Lot 1 in George F. Nixon & Company's Central Addition to Westchester, being a Subdivision ...

Also exactly because of Kenig's May 8, 2018 letter, we submitted into the record as an Exhibit the September 5, 2017 Cook County Assessor BUILDING RECORD RESIDENTIAL with the diagram of 1600 being totally attached to 1606 as:

"1600-1606 is ONE mixed-use building

Q-UP 2-12 4068#

When our Attorney argued that our real estate taxes had been reduced, Robles's answer was:

" So what."

Also exactly because of Kenig's May 8, 2018 letter, our Attorney submitted into the record for that June 19, 2019 hearing as demand by Byline four (4) actual pictures of the FOUR sides our actual totally attached 1600-1606:

1600-1606 is ONE mixed-use building

SEE: 1600-1606 Westchester Boulevard

Also exactly because of Kenig's May 8, 2018 letter, Exhibit 55 was our Exhibit for that June 19, 2019 hearing as demanded by Byline, a December 30, 2014 letter from the Village of Westchester as demanded by and provided to Byline for the 2015 renewals of our actual Loans with Byline:

The property located at 1606 Westchester Boulevard is zoned B-1 Office Business District. The property is improved with a one-story structure that has medical/dental offices and a residence on it. The structure was constructed in April 1954. The professional offices are currently permitted use. Residential uses are currently permitted above the first floor. The property is legal non-conforming with regard to the residential use on the first floor.

Exhibit 56 is the entirety of PLAINTIFF'S REPLY BRIEF IN SUPPORT OF ITS MOTION FOR APPOINTMENT OF A RECEIVER:

TWENTY-FOUR TIMES

TWO FRAUDULENTLY FABRICATED PHYSICALLY IMPOSSIBLE TWO SEPARATE BUILDINGS

SEE: 1600-1606 Westchester Boulevard

At that REPLY BRIEF:

"(h) The Village of Westchester considers the property to be one structure that has medical/dental offices and a residence on it.

"Contrary to the Borrowers' belief, the facts support the contention that the two buildings are separate and not on structure."

TWO FRAUDULENTLY FABRICATED PHYSICALLY IMPOSSIBLE SEPARATE BUILDINGS

SEE: FACTS/FIX

SEE: 1600-1606 Westchester Boulevard

Exhibit 57 is the cover sheet and the actual Plot Plan for our actual Property of the Restricted Appraisal Report for 1600-1606 Westchester Boulevard as dated January 12, 2019 and ordered by Kenig with Byline as an intended user which was Exhibit F of that REPLY BRIEF which also included five (5) actual pictures of our actual totally attached inseparable permanently bound custom built 1600-1606 as contained under one roof:

Property #1 (1600 Westchester Blvd.): A 2,845 SF, one-story over crawl space, attached medical office building with a detached garage.

ATTACHED

Property #2 (1606 Westchester Blvd.): A 1,320 SF, one-story over basement, attached single-family residence.

ATTACHED

ATTACHED: The term describing the physical union of two otherwise independent structures or objects; or the relationship between two parts of a single building, each having its own function.

Black's Law Dictionary

By that Restricted Appraisal Report as ordered by Kenig with Byline as an intended user, Kenig exactly evidenced that:

1600-1606 is ONE mixed-use building.

SEE: 1600-1606 Westchester Boulevard

Please note by that actual Plot Plan that our totally attached Westchester Medical Center is located entirely on PIN 15-21-301-206-0000; and our totally attached personal residence is located entirely on continuous PIN 15-21801-207-0000:

COOK COUNTY PARCEL NUMBERS ARE NOT LOT NUMBERS.

Further in that REPLY BRIEF:

The Sidwell map of Cook County, attached hereto as Exhibit E. also shows that the two buildings are on separate, distinct lots. The commercial building sits on Lot "206" and the residential building sits on Lot "207". A clearer picture of that same Sidwell map appears on Page 12 of the appraisal attached as Exhibit F.

Exhibit 4 herein is that actual **"Page 12"**.

Kenig exactly evidenced with that **"Page 12"** that our single story totally attached Westchester Medical Center is entirely located on the North 66.77 feet of Lot 1 and on PARCEL 206 for real estate taxation purposes only; and our single story totally attached personal residence is entirely located on the continuous South 34.23 feet of Lot 1 and on continuous PARCEL 207 for real estate taxation purposes.

Kenig's fraudulently misrepresented Sidwell map of Cook County" never existed; Kenig's fraudulently misrepresented "Exhibit E" never existed; Kenig's fraudulently fabricated separate "two buildings" could never have physically existed; Kenig's fraudulently fabricated "separate, distinct lots" could never have physically existed; Kenig's fraudulently fabricated separate "commercial building" could never have physically existed; Kenigs fraudulently fabricated separate and distinct "Lot 206" could never have physically existed; Kenig's fraudulently fabricated separate " residential building" could never have physically existed; and Kenig's fraudulently fabricated separate and distinct "Lot 207" could never have physically existed.

Kenig fraudulently misrepresented that actual PARCEL 206 for property taxation purposes only as that fraudulently fabricated separate and distinct "Lot 206" that could never have physically existed to fraudulently fabricate that separate "commercial building that could never have physically existed; and fraudulently misrepresented that actual continuous PARCEL 207 for property taxation purposes only as that fraudulently fabricated separate and distinct "Lot 207" that could never have physically existed to fraudulently fabricate that separate "residential building" that could never have physically existed; all for Kenig to forever fraudulently deny that LOT 1 ever existed:

COOK COUNTY PARCEL NUMBERS ARE NOT LOT NUMBERS

SEE: FACTS/FIX

SEE: 1600-1606 Westchester Boulevard

Further in that REPLY BRIEF:

"To support this argument, the Borrowers have attached four (4) pictures of the improvements on the property."

Those four (4) actual pictures and the five (5) actual pictures of 1600=1606 as attached to that Restricted Appraisal Report as ordered by Kenig to be prepared with Byline as an intended user actually depicted our totally attached inseparable permanently bound and contained under one roof as:

1600-1606 is ONE mixed-use building

SEE: 1600-1606 Westchester Boulevard

"Clearer pictures of the improvements are attached as Exhibits B and C. Exhibit B depicts the borrower's' personal residence and Exhibit C depicts the commercial building."

Exhibit 58 is Kenig's Exhibit B and Exhibit 59 is Kenig's **Exhibit C.**

Kenig's most absurd criminal fraudulently fabricated physically impossible fraud upon the court is that Kenig's picture of only the East side of 1600-1606 and then Kenig's picture of only the South side of 1600-1606 makes our totally attached custom built 1600-1606 Kenig's forever fraudulently fabricated physically impossible:

The Sidwell map of Cook County, attached hereto as Exhibit E, also shows that the two buildings are on separate, distinct lots. The commercial building sits on Lot "206" and the residential building sits on Lot "207".

Exhibit 60 is Page 13 of that Restricted Appraisal Report as ordered prepared by Kenig with Byline as an intended user:

Real Estate Tax Data (2017 taxes payable in 2008)

TAX PARCEL NUMBER	2017 REAL TAXES
Property #1	
15-21-301-206-0000	$6,643.29
15-21-301-209-0000	$1,264.53
Total	$7,907.80

Kenig exactly evidenced that our 2017 Assessment Appeal Number 0113329 did exist and was granted by the Cook County Assessor and that PARCEL 206 was reclassified by the Cook County Assessor as Class 2-12 to be assessed at 10% of market value:

SEE: FACTS/FIX

By that May 8, 2018 letter, Kenig fraudulently claimed that the 2017 Total Taxes for PARCEL 206 and PARCEL 209 would be $20,632.98 because PARCEL 206 was always Kenig's fraudulent misclassification of Class 517 to be assessed at 25% of market value.

The actual 2017 Total Tax for PARCEL 206 and PARCEL 209 is that $7,907.80 because the 2017 classification of PARCEL 206 is Class 2-12 to be assessed at 10% of market value:

SEE: FACTS/FIX

Exhibit 61 is the exact reason that Kenig had ordered the preparation of that fraudulently fabricated Restricted Appraisal Report with Byline as an intended user:

It is our opinion that the estimated "As is" value of Property #1, as of January 6, 2019 was:

TWO HUNDRED SEVENTY-THREE THOUSAND DOLLARS
$273,000.00

It is our opinion that the estimated "As is" value of Property #2 as of January 6, 2019 was:

ONE HUNDRED SIXTY-FIVE DOLLARS
$165,000.00

Kenig specifically ordered those fraudulently fabricated **"As is"** values to forever fraudulently deny that Byline and Kenig had caused the criminal fraudulent foreclosure of our actual Property for Byline to criminally seize our actual Property for vastly below its actual market value of $580,000.00.

INSTEAD, with that Restricted Appraisal Report as ordered by Kenig with Byline as an intended user Kenig ordered the exact evidence of all of Kenig's fraudulently fabricated physically impossible frauds upon the court before Kenig even committed Kenig's fraudulently fabricated physically impossible frauds upon the court.

Then Kenig will subsequently admit that on October 23, 2019 that the actual market value of our actual Property was $580,000.00 and therein defeat the exact reason that Kenig had ordered the preparation of that Restricted Appraisal Report with Byline as an intended user.

Kenig committed all of Kenig's fraudulently physically impossible frauds upon the court to forever fraudulently deny that PARCEL 206 was ever Class 2-12 to be assessed at 10% of market value but was always Kenig's fraudulent misclassification of Class 517 to always be assessed at 25 of market value; to forever fraudulently deny that Byline and Kenig had caused the criminal fraudulent foreclosure of our actual Property; because our actual totally attached custom built 1600-1606 always located on LOT 1 was always Kenig's fraudulently fabricated physically impossible:

The Sidwelt map of Cook County, attached hereto as Exhibit E, also shows that the two buildings are on separate, distinct lots. The commercial building sits on Lot "206" and the residential building sits on Lot "207".

COOK COUNTY PARCEL NUMBERS ARE NOT LOT NUMBERS

SEE: FACTS/FIX

SEE: 1600-1606 Westchester Boulevard

It is clear and well settled Illinois law that any attempt to commit fraud upon the court vitiates the entire proceeding: The People of the State of Illinois v. Fred E. Sterling; 357 Ill. 354 192 N.E. (1934): A court is without subject-matter jurisdiction and all of its order are void for reason of fraud upon the court: In re Village of Willowbrook; 357 Ill. App, (1962).

Under both Illinois and Federal law, when an officer of the court commits fraud upon the court during a proceeding, all orders and judgements of that court are void and of no legal force or effect.

AS EVIDENCED and as a MATTER OF LAW the entirety of 18 CH 13221 was already vitiated before that June 19, 2019 hearing as demanded by Byline and Kenig for the fraudulent procurement of that Receivership; Robles was never anything more than an evidenced criminal trespasser of the law with no subject-matter jurisdiction; and all of the orders and judgments to be criminally entered by Robles to aid and abet Byline in the criminal fraudulent foreclosure of our actual Property were already void and of no legal force or effect; for reason of Kenig's fraudulently fabricated physically impossible frauds upon the court; as exactly evidenced by Kenig before that June 19, 2019 hearing as demanded by Byline and Kenig for the fraudulent procurement of that Receivership.

SEE: 1600-1606 Westchester Boulevard

At that June 19, 2019 hearing after our Attorney had exactly evidenced:

My residence and the offices are contained in 1 building located on:

Lot 1 in George F. Nixon & Company's Central Addition to Westchester, being a Subdivision .....

Robles:

"Those are two buildings because they are on two lots."

That is exactly what then absolutely clueless Robles was told to say before that June 19, 2019 hearing as demanded by Byline and Kenig for the fraudulent procurement of that Receivership.

Exhibit 62 is the forever void fraudulently fabricated by Kenig physically impossible June 19, 2019 ORDER APPOINTING RECEIVERSHIP FOR NON-RESIDENTIAL PROPERTY as already prepared by Kenig before that June 19, 2019 hearing and then criminally entered by a then absolutely clueless Robles as a criminal trespasser of the law with no subject-matter jurisdiction:

Order Appointing Receiver - Form 20   4313; 4309; 4215

THE COURT FINDS:

2, The property is improved with a single-story medical office building that is owned by the defendants-mortgagors and is not for use as the defendants/mortgagor(s) personal residence.

Those were not **THE COURT FINDS** of Robles.

Those are the fraudulently fabricated by Kenig physically impossible THE COURT FINDS of Kenig as already prepared by Kenig before that June 19, 2019 hearing and then criminally entered by that then absolutely clueless Robles.

At the fraudulently fabricated by Kenig physically impossible PLAINTIFF'S MOTIOBN TO STRIKE

DEFENDANTS' COUNTERCLAIM FOR DAMAGES, Kenig, the maker of those June 19, 2019 THE COURT FINDS, was kind enough to explain to that then absolutely clueless Robles just exactly what Robles had criminally entered on that June 19, 2019:

After the dismissal of the bankruptcy, the Barretts, on several occasions, have expressed their dissatisfaction with the Court's ruling appointing a receivership by contending that the Court was wrong in finding that the 1600 property was separate from the 1606 Property.

That was never any **"court finding"** by then absolutely clueless Robles on that June 19, 2019.

What was criminally entered by then absolutely clueless Robles on that June 19, 2019 was Kenig's forever fraudulently fabricated physically impossible:

The Sidwell map of Cook County, attached hereto as Exhibit E, also shows that the two buildings are on separate, distinct lots. The commercial building sits on Lot "206" and the residential building sits on Lot "207".

COOK COUNTY PARCEL NUMBERS ARE NOT LOT NUMBERS

SEE: FACTS/FIX

SEE: 1600-1606 Westchester Boulevard

THAT IS THE FIX OF 18 CH 13221

Byline and Kenig just had then absolutely clueless Robles criminally enter whatever THE COURT FINDS of Kenig as put on front of Robles by Kenig: for then absolutely clueless Robles to also forever fraudulently deny that PARCEL 206 was ever Class 2-12 to be assessed at 10% of market value; but was always Kenig's fraudulent misclassification of Class 517 to always be assessed at 25% of market value; for Robles to also forever fraudulently deny that Byline and Kenig had caused the criminal foreclosure of our actual Property; because our actual single-story totally attached custom built 1600-1606 always located on LOT 1; was always Kenig's and now collusive Robles's fraudulently fabricated physically impossible:

The Sidwell map of Cook County, attached hereto as Exhibit E, also shows that the two buildings are on separate distinct lots. The commercial building sits on Lot "206" and the residential building sits on Lot "207".

COOK COUNTY PARCEL NUMBERS ARE NOT LOT NUMBERS

SEE: FACTS/FIX

SEE: 1600-1606 Westchester Boulevard

On July 1, 2019 the Receiver seized the rentals of our totally attached Westchester Medical Center by that fraudulently procured Receivership to squander those rentals with outrageous fees to further fraudulently prevent us from refinancing our actual Loans with Byline elsewhere.

On July 11, 2019 our Attorney filed our AFFIRMATIVE DEFENSE AND COUNTERCLAIM FOR DAMAGES citing the doctrine of unclean hands and Byline's fraudulent preparation of our actual real estate property tax escrow accounts as exactly evidenced by Kenig,

On July 15, 2019 we were criminally forced into Bankruptcy to avoid that fraudulently procured Receiver squandering our rentals with outrageous fees.

At the exact same time that Robles was criminally forcing us into Bankruptcy with that fraudulently procured Receivership, Exhibits 63 and 64 are the 2018 Cook County Treasurer Second Installment Property Tax Bills for PARCEL 206 and continuous PARCEL 207:

Classification 2-12

Those are the exact Cook County Treasurer property tax bills for PARCEL 206 and continuous PARCEL 207 that Byline and Kenig thought they had then absolutely clueless Robles already criminally FIX out of existence on June 19, 2019 to forever fraudulently deny that PARCEL 206 was ever Class 2-12 to be assessed at 10% of market value but was always Kenigs fraudulent misclassification of Class 517 to always be assessed at 25% of market value; for Robles to forever fraudulently deny that Byline and Kenig had caused the criminal foreclosure of our actual Property:

SEE: FACTS/FIX

Exhibit 65, as part of that criminal Bankruptcy, is the admission of Kenig:

Value of Property   **$580,000.00**

Then Kenig will forever fraudulently deny that the actual market value of our actual Property was ever that 580,000.00 to forever fraudulently deny that Byline and Kenig had caused the criminal fraudulent foreclosure of our actual Property for Byline to criminally seize our actual Property for vastly below that actual market value of that $580,000.00

At the September 2019 hearing at the Bankruptcy Trustee' office on Byline's MOTION to have our protection of that Bankruptcy dismissed with myself; my wife Darlene; our Attorney; Kenig' and the Bankruptcy Trustee in attendance:

Kenig: Alright Mr. Barrett, how much do you owe Byline Bank?

Myself: To be determined.

Kenig went NUCLEAR and started jumping up and down and screaming at me:

Kenig: NO. You cannot say that. You are under oath. You have to tell me how much you owe Byline Bank.

Trustee: Mr. Kenig, Mr. Barrett answered your question. Obviously, you do not like Mr. Barrett's answer, but it is Mr. Barrett's answer nonetheless. Now sit down and stop screaming.

Kenig: One more time and you are under oath. You have to tell me how much you owe Byline Bank.

Myself: To be determined. we filed our AFFIRMATIVE DEFENSE AND COUNTERCLAIM FOR DAMAGES.

Kenig went NUCLEAR again; started jumping up and down again and started screaming at the Trustee:

Kenig: NO. Tell Mr. Barrett that he has to tell me how much he owes Byline Bank.

Trustee: Mr. Kenig, if you do not sit down and stop screaming at me this meeting is over.

If I would have answered $400,00.00, we would have been out in the street the next day by Summary Judgement.

INSTEAD, because I answered "To be determined" Byline and Kenig and now a collusive Robles were stuck with fraudulently fabricated by Kenig physically impossible FIX of THE COURT FINDS of Kenig:

SEE: FACTS/FIX

Kenig committed fraud upon the Federal Bankruptcy Court of a fraudulently fabricated by Kenig **"tape recording"** that never existed to have our Bankruptcy proceeding fraudulently dismissed so Byline and Kenig could get back to now collusive Robles and the fraudulently fabricated by Kenig FIX of June 19, 2019 THE COURT FINDS of Kenig.

Kenig having done so, then Kenig immediately filed Byline's MOTION TO STRIKE DEFENDANTS MOTION FOR DAMAGES and MOTION TO STRIKE DEFENDANTS AFFIRMATIVE DEFENSES.

Just as immediately at ORDER ON PLAINTIFF"S MOTION TO STRIKE DEFENDANTS MOTION FOR DAMAGES and PLAINTIFF'S MOTION TO STRIKE DEFENDANTS' AFFIRMATIVE DEFENSES, Robles granted both MOTIONS to forever deny that Byline and Kenig had caused the criminal foreclosure of our actual Property because our actual totally attached custom built 1600-1606 always located entirely on LOT 1 was always Kenig's and now collusive Robles's fraudulently fabricated physically impossible:

The Sidwell map of Cook County, attached hereto as Exhibit E, also shows that the two buildings are on separate, distinct lots. The commercial building sits on Lot "206" and the residential building sits on Lot "207".

In doing so, Robles also ruled that we were not entitled to Byline' s records, for glaringly obvious reasons.

At the exact same time, Exhibits 66 and 67 are the 2018 Cook County Treasurer First Installment Property Tax Bills for LOT 1 and for PARCEL 206 and continuous PARCEL 207:

Classification 2-12

AGAIN, those are the exact actual Cook County Treasurer property tax bills for PARCEL 206 and continuous PARCEL 207 to be assessed at 10% of market value that first Byline and Kenig and now collusive Robles forever fraudulently deny ever existed; to forever fraudulently deny that Byline and Kenig had caused the criminal fraudulent foreclosure of our actual Property:

SEE: FACTS/FIX

At the exact same time that Robles was ruling that we were not entitled to Byline's records, for glaringly obvious reasons, Exhibit 68 as provided to us by Byline as part of the that criminal Bankruptcy proceeding is Byline's exact computer generated record for Note #11147585, the exact document we needed to prove that Byline and Kenig had caused the fraudulent foreclosure of our actual Property:

Loan Year-To-Date Activity

Note 111457585

Posting	Transaction	Escrow
END OF YEAR BALANCE		**$5,117.25**

There was never was any as fraudulently fabricated by Byline "Past Due Amount" nor any fraudulently fabricated by Byline "Escrow" due on September 21, 2018. There was never any as fraudulently fabricated by Kenig **"default"** in our actual real estate property tax escrow account for Note #11147585. Exhibit 68 as provided to us by Byline is the exact evidence that Byline and Kenig had fraudulently prevented us from refinancing our actual Loans with Byline elsewhere with that fraudulently fabricated September 6, 2018 criminal extortion of that $242,388.08 that we could not, did not, and would never pay.

SEE: FACTS/FIX

We had to disengage our Attorney who would be either disbarred or lose every case for the rest of his career for challenging the FIX of Kenig's THE COURT FINDS and we went Pro Se. Based upon the actual legal description of our actual Property; the actual pictures of our actual Property; the actual Classification 2-12 Cook County Treasure Property Tax Bills for PARCEL 206 and continuous PARCEL 207; and Byline's actual computer-generated records, we filed our MOTION TO VITIATE THE ENTIRE PROCEEDING AND VACATE ALL ORDERS FOR REASON OF PHYSICALLY IMPOSSIBLE FRAUDS UPON THE COURT.

INSTEAD: **The allegations against Plaintiff and Council seem to arise from a dispute about the amount of escrow payments that the Barretts were required to make under the loan documents versus what the Barretts were actually paying.**

No such fraudulently fabricated by Robles "dispute" ever existed.

As admitted by Wilson in that actual sham April 18, 2018 "demand letter" as prepared by Kenig no such **"dispute"** ever existed.

It appears that on or about April of 2018, the Barretts decided they were going to start making escrow payments less than the required amount under the loan documents.

As admitted by Wilson for Byline in that actual sham April 18, 2018 "demand letter" after our payment our February 16, 2018 payment of $3271.00 to Byline no further "escrow payments" were ever "required" of us by Byline under the actual provisions of Loan #11147585.

That, in part, led to a default letter being sent to the Barretts on April 18, 2018.

No such fraudulently fabricated by Robles April 18, 2018 "default letter" ever existed.

The words **"escrow"** never occurred in that actual sham April 18, 2018 "demand letter" as prepared by Kenig.

A letter dated May 8, 2018 from Plaintiff's counsel to the Barretts set forth in detail the reason that April 18, 2018 letter was sent.

No such fraudulently fabricated by Robles "reason" ever existed.

Specifically, the letter states that the default arose, in part, from the Barretts' "unilateral" decision to reduce the monthly tax escrow payments they were required to make under the loan documents from $1,671.45 down to $400.00 a month based upon the Barretts' efforts to have their properties reclassified from commercial to single mixed use.

No such fraudulently fabricated by Robles **"default"** in our actual real estate property tax escrow account for Loan #11147585 ever existed.

The already evidenced criminal conspiracy to defraud of Byline and Kenig to cause the criminal fraudulent foreclosure of our actual Property and now Robles's fraudulently fabricated criminal frauds upon the court are:

IDENTICAL

First Kenig and now collusive Robles fraudulently fabricated that entire April 18, 2018 "demand letter' that never existed; to then fraudulently fabricated that exact same "default" that never existed in our actual real estate property tax escrow account for Note #11157485; to forever fraudulently deny that Byline and Kenig had caused the criminal fraudulent foreclosure of our actual Property; to fraudulently fabricate that that the September 21, 2018 PAYOFF for Loan #1115845 was that fraudulently fabricated extortion of that $242,388.08 which we could not, did not, and would never pay:

SEE: FACTS/FIX

Further:

The issue of the alleged "misclassification" of the property as discussed by the Defendants does not establish a "fraudulent foreclosure" let alone defeat the instant foreclosure action. Though the Barretts MAY have achieved a reclassification of their

properties from commercial to "single mixed use"; the Court agrees with the Plaintiff that has nothing to do with the allegations in the complaint relating to the Barretts' alleged default under the loans in question. The reduction in tax liability that appears to have resulted from the Barretts' efforts to have the properties reclassified may be pertinent in calculating the nature the default, but has nothing to do with whether or not Defendant is in default as alleged or whether Plaintiff is entitled to file this foreclosure action based upon the alleged default in the complaint.

THAT IS THE FIX OF 18 CH13221

AS EVIDENCED by Kenig's fraudulently fabricated May, 8, 2018 letter, Byline and Kenig had caused the criminal fraudulent foreclosure of our actual Property by fraudulently preventing us from refinancing our actual Loans with Byline elsewhere with Kenig's forever fraudulent **"misclassification"** of PARCEL 206 always being Class 517 to be assessed at 25% of market value:

SEE: FACTS/FIX

AFTER Byline and Kenig having caused the criminal foreclosure of our actual Property with Kenig's forever fraudulent "misclassification" of PARCEL 206 always being Class 517 to be assessed at 25% of market value, then every word of Kenig's fraudulently fabricated physically impossible frauds upon the court forever fraudulently denied that PARCEL 206 was ever Class 2-12 to be assessed at 10% of market value but was always Kenig's forever fraudulent "misclassification" of Class 517 to always be assessed at 25% of market value to forever fraudulently deny that Byline and Kenig had caused the criminal foreclosure of our actual Property.

NOW, the criminal conspiracy of Byline and Kenig and now collusive Robles is that Kenig's forever fraudulent **"misclassification"** of PARCEL 206 always being Class 517 to always be assessed at 25% of market value did not cause the criminal foreclosure of our actual Property:

SEE: FACTS/FIX

That MOTION, and all of our MOTIONS TO RECONSIDER will always suffer the same fate:

"Again, the Defendants have simply failed to establish, by evidence, that a genuine issue of material fact existed at the time the judgement was entered, or exists today that a finding that Plaintiff is entitled to judgement as matter of law as to Note I and II as alleged in Plaintiff's Amended Complaint. The Courts' prior findings of fact and rulings in this matter stand. The Barretts have failed to carry the burden in the instant motion to reconsider, therefore, the motion is DENIED in its entirety.

AS EVIDENCED and as a MATTER OF LAW, both state and Federal, the entirety of 18 CH 13221 was vitiated before that June 19, 2019 hearing as demanded by Byline and Kenig for the fraudulent procurement of that Receivership; Robles was never anything more than an evidenced criminal trespasser of the law with no subject-matter jurisdiction; and all of Robles criminally entered Orders and Judgements to aid and abet Byline in the criminal foreclosure of our actual Property as caused by Kenig; for Byline to criminally seize our actual Property for vastly below its actual market value of $580,000.00 were already void and of no legal force or effect before that June 19, 219 hearing as demanded by Byline for the fraudulent procurement of that Receivership; for reason of Kenig's fraudulently fabricated physically impossible frauds upon the court; as evidenced by Kenig before that June 19, 2019 hearing as demanded by Byline for the fraudulent procurement of that Receivership.

At the exact same in 2020 and 2021:

Exhibit 69 and Exhibit 70 are the Cook County Treasurer 2019 Second Installment Property Tax Bill for PARCEL 206 and continuous PARCEL 207:

Classification 2-12

Exhibit 71 and Exhibit 72 are the Cook County Treasurer 2020 First Installment Property Tax Bills for PARCEL 206 and continuous PARCEL 207:

Classification 2-12

Exhibit 73 and Exhibit 74 are the Cook County Treasurer 2021 Second Installment Property Tax Bills for PARCEL 206 and PARCEL 207:

Classification 2-12

Those are the exact Classification 2-12 property tax bills for PARCEL 206 and continuous PARCEL 207 to be assessed at 10% of market value that first Byline and Kenig and now collusive Robles forever fraudulently deny ever existed to forever fraudulently deny that Byline and Kenig had caused the criminal foreclosure of our actual Property:

SEE: FACTS/FIX

At the December 27, 2021 fraudulently fabricated by Kenig physically impossible PLAINTIFF'S RESPONSE BRIEF IN SUPPORT OF ITS MOTION FOR SUMMARY JUDGEMENT, Kenig, the maker of the fraudulently fabricated physically impossible June 19, 2019 THE COURT FINDS of Kenig, will further explain to now collusive Robles just exactly what that then absolutely clueless Robles criminally entered on that June 19, 2019:

Receivership Order:

The majority of Barretts' Response and Addendum continues to rehash the Barretts' dissatisfaction with this Court's entry of the Receivership Order, which was outlined

above, is long since moot. While the Barretts continue to think that the 1600 Property and the 1606 Property are one building, the Court, long ago, based on the facts presented to this Court at the Receivership hearing concluded that the 1600 Property and the 1606 Property are two separate buildings, with the former being occupied by commercial tenants and the latter consisting of the Barretts' personal residence.

What was criminally entered on that June 19, 2019 by then absolutely clueless Robles was Kenig's forever fraudulently fabricated physically impossible:

The Sidwell map of Cook County, attached hereto as Exhibit E, also shows that the two buildings are on separate, distinct lots. The commercial building sits on Lot "206" and the residential building sits on Lot "207".

COOK COUNTY PARCEL NUMBERS ARE NOT LOT NUMBERS

SEE: 1600-1606 Westchester Boulevard

Exhibit 75 is the forever void February 10, 2022 ORDER as already prepared by Kenig and then criminally entered by Robles as never anything more than an evidenced criminal trespasser of the law with no subject-matter jurisdiction.

Byline is criminally granted summary judgment on **EVERYTHING**;

Robles ordered the criminal public auction of our actual Property;

A summary judgment against us is criminally granted to Byline in the amount of $457,976.33;

And we have to pay Kenig's legal fees in the amount of $80,766.80;

All because our actual totally attached custom built 1600-1606 always located on LOT 1 was always first Kenig's and now collusive Robles's forever fraudulently fabricated physically impossible:

The Sidwell map of Cook County, attached hereto as Exhibit E, also shows that the two buildings are on separate, distinct lots. The commercial building sits on Lot "206" and the residential building sits on Lot "207".

At the JUDGEMENT OF FORECLOSURE OF SALE as prepared by Kenig:

(1600 Westchester Boulevard, Westchester, Illinois)

PARCEL 1:

LOT 1 EXCEPT THE SOUTH 34.23 FEET .....

PIN No. 15-21-301-206-0000

That is the exact evidence of first Kenig's and then collusive Robles's fraudulently fabricated physically impossible:

The Sidwell map of Cook County, attached hereto as Exhibit E, also shows that the two buildings are on two separate, distinct lots. The commercial building sits on Lot "206" and the residential building sits on Lot "207".

COOK COUNTY PARCEL NUMBERS ARE NOT LOT NUMBERS

SEE: FACTS/FIX

SEE: 1600 -1606 Westchester Boulevard

At JUDGEMENT AND FORECLOSURE OF SALE as also prepared by Kenig.

(1606 Westchester Boulevard, Westchester, Illinois 60154)

THE SOUTH 34.23 FEET OF LOT 1 ....

PIN No. 15-21-301-207-0000

That is also the exact evidence of first Kenig's and then now collusive Robles's fraudulently fabricated physically impossible:

The Sidwell map of Cook County, attached hereto as Exhibit E, also shows that the two buildings are located on two separate, distinct lots. The commercial building sits on Lot "206" and the residential building sits on Lot "207".

COOK COUNTY PARCEL NUMBERS ARE NOT LOT NUMBERS

SEE: FACTS/FIX

SEE: 1600-1606 Westchester Boulevard

At the same time, Exhibit 76 and Exhibit 77 are the 2021 Cook County Treasurer First Installment Property Tax Bills for PARCEL 206 and continuous PARCEL 207:

Classification 2-12

Those are the Classification 2-12 property tax bills that first Byline and Kenig and then now collusive Robles forever fraudulently deny ever existed to forever fraudulently deny that Byline and Kenig had caused the criminal foreclosure of our actual Property.

AT LAW, every Judicial Sale must include the legal description and the Property Index Number of the Property being auctioned.

Exhibit 78 is the NOTICE OF SALE dated May 16, 2022 for the criminal public auction of our actual

Property to be criminally arranged by Kenig:

PARCEL 1:

LOT 1 EXCEPT THE SOUTH 34.23 ....

PIN No. 15-21-301-206-0000

PARCEL 2:

THE SOUTH 34.23 FEET OF LOT 1 ....

PIN No. 15-21-301-207-0000

Robles had been warned, numerous times, that if Robles proceeded with the criminal fraudulent foreclosure of our actual Property as caused by Byline and Kenig that the actual legal description our actual Property would exactly evidence first Kenig's and then collusive Robles's fraudulently fabricated physically impossible:

The Sidwell map of Cook County, attached hereto as Exhibit E, also shows that the two buildings are on separate, distinct lots. The commercial building sits on Lot "206" and the residential building sits on Lot "207".

SO WHAT

SEE: FACTS/FIX

Byline won the criminal fraudulent public auction of our actual Property as fraudulently arranged by Kenig with a bid of $395,250, vastly below the actual market value of our actual Property of $580,000.00.

Exhibit 79 as already prepared by Kenig and then criminally entered by Robles on December 19, 2022 as nothing more than an evidenced by Kenig criminal trespasser of the law with no subject-matter jurisdiction is the forever void ORDER APPROVING REPORT OF SALE, CONFIRMING SALE, AND ORDER OF POSSESSION:

LOT 1 EXCEPT THE SOUTH 34.23 FEET ....

PIN No. 15-21=301-206-0000

THE SOUTH 34.23 FEET OF LOT 1 .....

PIN No. 15-21-301-207-0000

That is the exact evidence of first Kenig's and then collusive Robles's forever fraudulently fabricated physically impossible:

The Sidwell map of Cook County, attached hereto as Exhibit E, also shows that the two buildings are on separate, distinct lots. The commercial building sits on Lot "206" and the residential building sits on Lot "207".

COOK COUNTY PARCEL NUMBERS ARE NOT LOT NUMBERS

SEE: FACTS/FIX

SEE: 1600-1606 Westchester Boulevard

The real property located at 1600 Westchester Boulevard, Westchester, Illinois 60154 that is the subject matter of this proceeding consists of a one-story office building with on-site parking and a garage and the real property located at 1606 Westchester Boulevard, Westchester, Illinois 60154 that is also the subject matter of this proceeding consists of a one-story single-family residence (collectively the "Properties").

"Properties"

That is first Kenig's and then now collusive Robles's forever fraudulently physically impossible:

The Sidwell map of Cook County, attached hereto as Exhibit E, also shows that the two buildings are located on separate, distinct lots. The commercial building sits on Lot "206" and the residential building sits on Lot "207".

COOK COUNTY PARCEL NUMBERS ARE NOT LOT NUMBERS

SEE: FACTS/FIX

SEE: 1600-1606 Westchester Boulevard

Byline is granted possession of our actual Property; a net deficiency judgement of $170,522.01 is granted against us; and the Sheriff is ordered to evict us from our home all because our actual totally attached custom built 1600-1606 always located on LOT 1 was always first Kenig's and now collusive Robles's forever fraudulently fabricated physically impossible:

The Sidwell map of Cook County, attached hereto as Exhibit E, also shows that the two buildings are located on separate distinct lots. The commercial building sits on Lot "206" and the residential building sits on Lot "207".

We filed our Motion to Reconsider AND a Counterclaim for Damages in the amount of $5,000,000.00 based upon the actual legal description of our actual Property: the actual pictures of our actual Property; the actual Cook County Treasurer Property Tax Bills for PARCEL 206 and continuous PARCEL 207; and Byline's actual computer-generated records as provided by Kenig.

INSTEAD, Exhibit 80 is the culmination of Robles's years of criminally aiding and abetting Byline in the criminal fraudulent foreclosure of our actual Property; as caused by Kenig's forever fraudulent misclassification of PARCEL 206 always being Class 517 to always be assessed at 25% of market value; for Byline to criminally seize our actual Property for vastly below its actual market of $580,000.00:

However, even if it had met pleading standards and filed by /5/2021, the Court finds that the prposed counterclaim is factually unsupported by evidence adduced and legally deficient. Therefore, the Defendants' motion is DENIED.

EVIDENCE

AS EVIDENCED and as a MATTER OF LAW, both State and Federal, the entire proceeding of 18 CH13221 was already vitiated before that June 19, 2019 hearing as demanded by Byline for the fraudulent procurement of that Receivership; Robles was never anything more than an evidenced. Criminal trespasser of the law with no subject matter jurisdiction; and all of Robles's ORDERS and Judgements as criminally entered to aid and abet Byline in the criminal fraudulent foreclosure of our actual Property as caused by Kenig's forever fraudulent misclassification of PARCEL 206 always being Class 517 to be assessed at 25% of market value; for Bylne to criminally seize our actual Property for vastly below its actual market value of $580,000.00; were already void and of no legal force or effect before that June 19, 2019 hearing as demanded by Byline for the fraudulent procurement of that Receivership; for reason of Kenig's fraudulently fabricated physically impossible frauds upon the court; as exactly evidenced by Kenig in the filed record before that June 19, 2019 hearing as demanded by Byline for the fraudulent procurement of that Receivership.

SEE: FACTS/FIX

SEE: 1600-1606 Westchester Boulevard

Exhibit 81 is Kenig's PLAINTIFF'S RESPONSE TO DEFENDANTS' MOTION TO RECONSIDER THE COURT ORDER APPROVING REPORT OF SALE AND DISTRIBUTION, CONFIRMING SALE AND ORDER OF POSSESSION in its entirety as the exact evidence of Kenig's FIVE YEARS of fraudulently fabricated physically impossible frauds upon the court:

The Barretts again complain about the Court's long ago entry of the order of receivership and their mistaken belief that the subject properties are one mixed use building. On 26 different occasions throughout their Motion, the Barretts state:

"TWO FRAUDULENTLY FABRICATED PHYSICALLY IMPOSSIBLE SEPARATE BUILDINGS" as if to convince this Court that it was wrong for appointing a receivership as to the property located at 1600 Westchester Boulevard. And virtually all of the exhibits attached to the motion relate strictly to the false narrative that the two properties are in fact one building.

The Restricted Appraisal Report was ordered by Byline in connection with the filing of the lawsuit on October 23, 2018. It was attached as Exhibit F to Byline's reply brief in support of its motion to appoint a receiver filed on May 29, 2019. The Restricted Appraisal Report was attached to the reply brief for the sole purpose of supporting Byline's argument that the subject property contained two buildings and two separate lots for the purpose of Byline's motion to appoint receiver for one of the buildings.

Exhibit B attached hereto shows that the Restricted Appraisal Report was requested by Byline.

Specially the reply brief stated:

The Sidwell map of Cook County, attached hereto as Exhibit E, also shows that the two buildings are on separate, distinct lots. The commercial building sits on Lot "206" and the residential building sits on Lot "207".

COOK COUNTY PARCEL NUMBERS ARE NOT LOT NUMBERS

SEE: FACTS/FIX

SEE: 1600-1606 Westchester Boulevard

Exhibit 82 is Kenig's **"Exhibit B":**

Property #1 (1600 Westchester Blvd.): A 2,845 SF, 1-story over crawl space, attached medical office building with a detached garage.

ATTACHED

Property #2 (1606 Westchester Blvd.): A 1,320 SF, 1-story over basement, attached single-family residence.

ATTACHED

ATTACHED: The term describing the physical union of two otherwise independent structures or objects; or the relationship between two parts of a single structure; each having its own function.

Black's Law Dictionary

1600-1606 is ONE mixed-use building

SEE: 1600-1606 Westchester Boulevard

At our DEFENDANTS' RESPONSE TO PLAINTIFF'S TO DEFENDANTS' MOTION TO RECONSIDER:

THIS IS THE STUPIDEST FIX IN THE HISTORY OF COOK COUNTY IN PLAIN SIGHT FOR ALL TO SEE

SEE: 1600-1606 Westchester Boulevard

"My residence and the offices are contained in 1 building located on:

Lot 1 in George F. Nixon & Company's Central Addition to Westchester, being a Subdivision ...

1600-1606 is ONE mixed-use building

SEE: 1600-1606 Westchester Boulevard

The Sidwell map of Cook County, attached hereto as Exhibit E, also that the two buildings are on separate, distinct lots. The commercial building sits on Lot "206" and the residential building sits on Lot "207".

COOK COUNTY PARCEL NUMBERS ARE NOT LOT NUMBERS

SEE: FACTS/FIX

SEE: 1600-1606 Westchester Boulevard

Truth shall spring from the earth and righteousness shall look down from heaven.

Psalm 85: 11-12

LOT 1